A Garden A Day

A Garden A Day

Ruth Chivers

First published in the United Kingdom in 2023 by
B. T. Batsford Books Limited
43 Great Ormond Street
London WC1N 3HZ
An imprint of B. T. Batsford Books Limited

ISBN: 9781849947893

A CIP catalogue record for this book is available
from the British Library.

30 29 28 27 26 25 24 23
10 9 8 7 6 5 4 3 2 1

Reproduction by Rival Colour Ltd, UK
Printed by Toppan Leefund Printing Ltd, China

This book can be ordered direct
from the publisher at the website:
www.batsford.com, or try your
local bookshop.

Page one: Bright planting at Charleston (see
page 225) in East Sussex, England.

Previous spread: Charles Dowding's vegetable
garden is filled with abundant produce in
autumn (see page 322).

Right: Barnsley House's magnificent laburnum
walk (see page 155) is at its best in late spring.

Opposite: Arundel Castle's Tulip Festival (see
page 109) is celebrated in April and early May.

CONTENTS

INTRODUCTION

Right: The Lost
Gardens of
Heligan (see page
270) retain an air
of mystery.

Below: *Des Gouttes
de Pluie* by Spanish
artist Samuel
Salcedo is at Les
Jardins d'Etretat
(see page 88).

The importance of easy access to nature has been highlighted
in recent years. Having your own slice of nature in a garden
outside your home is a valuable resource. Gardens have been created
in different ways across the major global cultures since ancient
times. As cultivated outdoor spaces, they are universally places for
reflection and recreation, safe havens from the outside world beyond
their boundaries – a world that is beyond control.

Selecting gardens for this book prompted exploration of a number
of underlying questions including: What is a garden? What are
gardens for? What makes a garden? Why do we make gardens?

All gardens are artificial – even those that look the most
naturalistic are created by interventions with nature. The basic raw

Above: Prospect
Cottage garden
(see page 58),
Derek Jarman's
legacy, is defined
by colourful
plants, flintstone
details and
driftwood against
the shingle
expanse of
Dungeness, Kent.

Opposite:
The timeless
quality of Villa
Vignamaggio
(see page 38)
makes the perfect
backdrop to any
garden scene.

materials to make any size or type of garden are simple: stone and
water, with trees, grass and other plants dependent on climate and
location. Using these same ingredients in different proportions
results in a remarkable diversity of garden styles that are influenced
by cultural legacy and history. Allocating gardens to different
categories broadened research and selection beyond boundaries and
borders, both real and metaphorical.

Apart from well-known gardens, other aims were to include
fictional gardens, artists' and writers' gardens, historic and modern
gardens, gardens where significant events have taken place, and to
acknowledge the contribution of plant hunters. While all gardens
are ephemeral in one sense, their ability to inspire creativity is long-
lasting and their flexibility means they can be used in ways that reflect
changing times. The aim was to make most entry dates reflect the
stories behind a garden and also (where practical) to follow seasonal
changes of appearance that are most apparent in many gardens.

For hundreds of years, gardens have been acknowledged as healing
spaces that inspire mental well-being ,as well as places for all ages
to play. I aimed to separate the enjoyment and pleasure of being
in a garden from the physical activity of gardening, which may be
therapeutic for some, but is not everyone's choice for connecting

with the natural world in a beneficial way – and leaves out those
without their own gardens or access to a shared community growing
space. Visiting a garden and spending time in a cared-for outdoor
space brings the same uplifting benefits and improves mental health
without the responsibilities of ownership.

Enclosed gardens have a particularly enduring appeal. For many
centuries and across different cultures, they have represented
paradise on earth. 'Paradise' has its roots in a Persian/Iranian word
modified by the ancient Greeks to '*paradeisos*', translated as 'enclosed
park', and the term is still used today by people creating their own
private versions. Walls were essential in gardens of the ancient
world to keep the dangers of the natural wild world out and create
a safe, private haven within. But gardens of all types inspire positive
emotions and can console and comfort in dark and stressful times.

Gardens are about the people who created them and the reasons
why they made them look as they do. I have tried to reflect this in this
book, and to also focus on the idea that gardens are for people to enjoy.

Above: Gordon
Castle Walled
Garden (see pages
218–9) has plenty
of space for an
abundance of
colourful flowers
alongside edible
produce.

Opposite:
RHS Garden
Bridgewater,
Salford,
Manchester,
England (see
page 321)

11

AN ENGLISH CALENDAR (1938), EVELYN DUNBAR
The Garden Personified

Evelyn Dunbar's
*An English
Calendar* (1938)
was the painter's
largest piece to
date.

New Year's Day has only been celebrated on this day in Britain since 1752, when the country finally adopted the 'new' Gregorian calendar of 1582 to bring the country in line with most other European countries.

Making plans for the seasons ahead is a constant with gardeners. Artist Evelyn Dunbar was also a skilled gardener. This large painting resembles a calendar in a medieval book of hours; each month is personified according to general gardening tasks and events. Female figures are allocated to months where work is lighter, with more floral displays, while men are burdened with the months where gardening requires more utilitarian tasks, perhaps displaying the artist's gentle sense of humour. Seasons have been personified since ancient times. Each affects a garden's appearance, but nature dictates their arrival and end, rather than fixed calendar dates.

The gardening year 'proper' does not really start until later, but in the depths of winter it is good to look ahead to a joyful spring and beyond.

ALHAMBRA AND GENERALIFE, GRANADA, SPAIN
Magnificent Castle Gardens

The central fountain inside the Court of the Lions, as seen from inside the intricately carved colonnades.

The Alhambra and Generalife comprise a whole hilltop of planted terraces, courtyards and water gardens. This series of Islamic representations of earthly paradise demonstrates the horticultural skills of the Moorish dynasty that ruled this part of Spain from the 13th century to the late 15th century. The last Moorish ruler of Spain, Boabdil, surrendered to Castilian forces on this day in 1492.

The famed Court of the Lions (*Patio de los Leones*) takes its name from stone lions supporting the fountain at the centre of the traditional Islamic *chahar bagh* – a design defined by rills of water that divide the courtyard into four quarters. It is a calm, cool space in intense summer heat.

WILD GARDEN, WINTER (1959), JOHN NASH
A Garden in Watercolour

Wild Garden, Winter, (watercolour on paper, 1959), John Nash. John had no formal art training but was encouraged by his brother, Paul.

Artist John Nash captures the stark beauty of his wintry garden at Bottengoms, Essex, in this watercolour. Twisted tree trunks take on sculptural qualities, bare branches become delicate tracery and ice shimmers on the frozen pond. Nash was a keen gardener and plantsman, inspired by landscape and nature. He was known for his botanical studies of wild and garden flowers and was a judge at the RHS Chelsea Flower Show. His short memoir *The Artist Plantsman* recounted his childhood love of gardens and plants; commissioned work included *English Garden Flowers*, and illustrations for *Plants with Personality* and *The Curious Gardener*.

Nash was an official war artist in both the First and Second World War, as was his brother, Paul Nash.

20 FORTHLIN ROAD, LIVERPOOL, ENGLAND
The Garden that Birthed The Beatles

Paul McCartney's home and front garden as it was when he lived there in the 1960s.

Paul McCartney moved to this home in his early teens. The ordinary-looking terraced house played a pivotal role in McCartney's early career, including when he met John Lennon. McCartney's family lived here for nine years, during which McCartney and Lennon wrote songs and rehearsed here (see page 284).

Gardens are bound up with a sense of home. Front gardens signal the everyday changes of season and weather. They are part of every departure and homecoming, however ordinary or extraordinary those events may be.

TWELFTH NIGHT (1601–2), WILLIAM SHAKESPEARE
Hiding in a Box

This 1968 cover of Shakespeare's *Twelfth Night* shows Malvolio amongst the box hedges.

Maria: *Get ye all three into the box-tree: Malvolio's coming down this walk. He has been yonder i' the sun practising behaviour to his own shadow this half-hour.*

TWELFTH NIGHT, ACT II, SCENE V

Shakespeare's *Twelfth Night* or *What You Will* is a love triangle comedy. A garden presents excellent opportunities for concealment in places where conversations can be overheard.

Sir Toby, Sir Andrew and Fabian hide in a 'box-tree' to observe the reactions of the pompous, disagreeable Malvolio to a forged letter written to trick him into thinking Olivia is in love with him. Evergreen box – *Buxus sempervirens* – has been planted in gardens since ancient times, particularly as hedges and for creating topiary shapes. It provides year-round structure, and opportunities for concealing anything that needs to be hidden.

GOTANJYOU-JI TEMPLE, TAKEFU, JAPAN
A Modern Zen Garden

This exceptional contemporary garden respects the traditions of Japanese garden design. It invites reflection, while its paths make a functional link between buildings.

Shunmyo Masuno designs gardens as part of his practice as a monk, following the tradition of Zen priests, who express part of their ascetic practice through the art of landscape design. At Gotanjyou-ji temple in 2009, he designed a modern garden based on classical principles of Japanese garden design as a tribute to Keizan Zenji, a 13th-century Zen priest.

All elements invite reflection. Organically shaped moss-covered mounds define the ground. Plant and rock placement is considered. One large upright rock represents Keizan Zenji, whose spread of Zen teaching throughout the country is symbolized by the gravel stream.

HP (HEWLETT-PACKARD) GARAGE, PALO ALTO, CALIFORNIA, USA
Garden Birthplace of Silicon Valley

The garage where Silicon Valley was born is now part of a private museum viewable only from the sidewalk and driveway.

This garden and garage were dedicated as the birthplace of Silicon Valley in 1989. Fifty years earlier, David Packard and his wife rented an apartment in the small house, chosen specifically because it had a garage. Friend Bill Hewlett moved into the garden shed. The two men worked together part-time and the garage became their development lab and workshop. Many products were developed here, including their first, an audio oscillator.

Their partnership was soon formalized into Hewlett-Packard Company and moved into larger premises close by. The garage became a California Historical Landmark in 1987. It remained privately owned until the HP company bought the entire site in 2000. It was listed on the National Register of Historic Places in 2007. Many businesses start in gardens, but not all go on to achieve a global presence.

HODSOCK PRIORY, NOTTINGHAMSHIRE, ENGLAND
A Snow-White Blanket

Hodsock Priory's 2ha (5ac) of garden and around 5ha (12ac) of woodland are blanketed by snowdrops in January and February, and bluebells in April.

There's something about snowdrops that turns many people into galanthophiles, as enthusiasts for the delicate little flowers are called. The ordinary form, *Galanthus nivalis*, emerges through snow and the general leaf and twig debris of winter to carpet expanses of ground with pure white flowers with a touch of pale green at their centres.

Hodsock Priory is a historic country house that has never been a priory, despite its name. The garden is estimated to have some four million snowdrops. Combined with yellow aconites and lilac-rose cyclamen, they turn swathes of ground into a beautiful carpet of winter colour.

'COUNTRY GARDENS', ENGLISH FOLK TUNE
'In an English Country Garden'

Percy Grainger seated at the piano. He was renowned for his energetic approach to life. He often ran to concert venues with a rucksack on his back and was fluent in 11 languages.

Australian-born composer and musician Percy Grainger arranged this old English folk tune in 1918. The tune was collected by Cecil Sharp, founding father of the revival of English folk dance and song. 'Country Gardens' was Grainger's most famous work, his calling card and an essential item on his concert programmes. His arrangement broke its publisher's record for 75 consecutive years. It was written when he was living in the USA; having moved there in 1914, he spent the rest of his life in America.

'Country Gardens' reached No. 5 in the UK charts in June 1962 for singer Jimmie F. Rogers – an unlikely hit in the Swinging Sixties.

CHÂTEAU DE CHEVERNY, LOIRE VALLEY, FRANCE
Captain Haddock's Garden, Marlinspike Hall

The south facade of Château de Cheverny, the inspiration behind Captain Haddock's home. The first Tintin comic strip, a serialization of *Tintin in the Land of the Soviets*, was released on 10th January 1929.

Tintin fans know that his friend Captain Haddock's ancestral home is Marlinspike Hall, the English translation of Château de Moulinsart in the original text. Cartoonist Hergé used the name of a real village in his native Belgium, despite the fact that Haddock is English. Even more confusing is that Hergé's illustrations show the front garden of the Château de Cheverny in the Loire Valley, minus the wings to each side of the house. No mention is made of who keeps Haddock's – or should that be Hadoque's? – French-style lawn trimmed in his prolonged absences. Cheverny has a permanent exhibition devoted to the adventures of Tintin and his friend.

GARDEN COVE (1948–50), IVON HITCHENS
A Garden Without Boundaries

*Garden Cove
(oil on canvas,
1948-50), Ivon
Hitchens*

This garden has no boundary with the landscape beyond and is not structured by traditional borders within. Artist Ivon Hitchens moved to a caravan on this site in 1940 when his London home was bombed. He had previously bought over 2ha (6ac) of woodland near Petworth, Sussex. Greenleaves, his home on the left of the painting, was built over a number of years as he extended his land holdings. The garden appears to engulf the house; together with the surrounding landscape, it provided constant inspiration for Hitchens' paintings.

SKY GARDEN, 20 FENCHURCH STREET, LONDON, ENGLAND
A Garden 150 Metres Up

From Sky Garden you can see landmarks such as the Shard, St. Paul's Cathedral, Tower Bridge and the London Eye.

Sky Garden is London's highest public garden. Its glass structure sits on the top three floors of the building that has become known as the Walkie Talkie – a curvaceous structure designed by Uruguayan architect Rafael Viñoly. Lush planting weaves through observation decks and an open-air terrace, all with panoramic views. The planted terraces feature a variety of Mediterranean and South African species.

THE GARDENER'S LABYRINTH (1577), DYDYMUS MOUNTAINE
An Elizabethan Garden Book

This illustration on the title page of the first edition shows the creation of a bower – the forerunner of the pergola.

Thomas Hill was an astrologer who also worked as a translator and compiler for a book printer. *The Gardener's Labyrinth*, published in 1577 after Hill's death c.1574, was the first substantial book in English on gardening and garden design. Published under Dydymus Mountaine, a Latin pseudonym of Hill's real name, the text actually comprised a collection of the writings of other authors – as Hill states on the title page, 'Gathered out of the best approved writers of Gardening, Husbandrie, and Physicke'.

Illustrations provide us with knowledge of the gardens of the wealthier Elizabethans as places for decorative display and pleasure in addition to growing fruit, vegetables and herbs. Decorative features, such as mazes, arbours and pleached trained trees, are shown in the book and are also mentioned by Shakespeare.

ALICE'S ADVENTURES IN WONDERLAND (1865), LEWIS CARROLL
A Strange Garden Party

John Tenniel's woodcut illustration for the first edition of *Alice's Adventures in Wonderland* invites us to this tea party.

'It's the stupidest tea-party I ever was at in all my life!'

ALICE, *ALICE'S ADVENTURES IN WONDERLAND*

The Mad Hatter's tea party is one of the most famous garden parties in literature. It's not like any garden party the real Alice would have encountered. Tea is taken at six o'clock, the time at which the Mad Hatter is perpetually stuck following an unfortunate encounter with the Queen of Hearts.

There is plenty of space, but Alice is not welcomed. A barrage of riddles with no answers, confusing stories and rude personal remarks cause her to leave, vowing never to return. It's not the genteel experience usually associated with afternoon garden tea parties.

ARCTIC-ALPINE BOTANIC GARDEN, TROMSØ, NORWAY
Arctic Colour

At 320km (200 mi) inside the Arctic Circle, this is the most northerly botanic garden in the world. Its plant collections come from areas across the world where species grow in similar cool, rocky conditions. Tromsø benefits from the warming Gulf Stream, but one day climate change may affect this. Plants need to cope with lower light levels, as from November until mid-January the sun doesn't appear above the horizon. Flowering starts in May and lasts until the first snow, usually in October.

'FOLLIES', WALLPAPER, MANSFIELD PARK COLLECTION, OSBORNE & LITTLE
A Wallpaper Garden 1

This wallpaper design turns a single wall into a visual illusion garden, a *trompe l'oeil* of many different features. False perspective paths add depth to the mixture of classical statues, fountains, garden ornaments, gazebos, stone balustrades, topiary, trained trees and traditional striped lawns.

RYŌAN-JI, KYOTO, JAPAN
Zen Dry Landscape Garden

Above: The Ryōan-ji garden is a UNESCO World Heritage Site.

Opposite top: This garden has no fences; plants meld with native vegetation beyond its boundaries.

Opposite bottom: It's a challenge to count how many different garden-related things are in view.

Zen temple courtyards made from dry raked gravel are known as *kare-sansui* – dry landscape gardens – and this is the most famous in Japan. The wall encloses 15 rocks of different sizes set in immaculately raked gravel. Nothing detracts or distracts from contemplation.

Some attribute its design to 16th-century landscape painter Sōami, while others believe it is the work of an unknown master. Ryōan-ji, the Peaceful Dragon Temple, has survived for more than 500 years. On its site is a large pond dating from the 12th century. Over the years, different priests have planted trees such as cherries and maples, along its banks.

WAKEHURST PLACE GARDEN AND MILLENNIUM SEED BANK, ARDINGLY, WEST SUSSEX, ENGLAND
The Winter Garden

Wakehurst's Winter Garden features over 33,000 different plants of various textures and hues.

Royal Botanic Gardens, Kew (see page 275) have managed Wakehurst and its magnificent plant collections since 1965. This Winter Garden's bold contemporary planting shows the diversity of colour, texture and touches of early fragrance that give garden interest through the coldest months. Snow-white trunks of West Himalayan birch (*Betula utilis* var. *jacquemontii*) shine among swathes of red- and yellow-stemmed dogwoods and willows. Low-growing evergreen perennials and grasses carpet the space around trees and shrubs. Snowdrops and lilac cyclamen add early flower colour from January onwards.

Hidden underneath Wakehurst, the Millennium Seed Bank holds a collection of over 2.4 billion seeds from around the world, the world's largest collection of seeds from wild plant species. It is a secure, state-of-the-art research facility.

MODEL OF AN EGYPTIAN GARDEN AND PORCH (C.1981–75 BCE)
A Model Garden

Models of ancient Egyptian gardens show the features considered to be essential to enjoyment of a garden space.

This modern-looking model garden was found on the side panel of the tomb of Meketre in Thebes. Meketre was a royal chief steward who served Egyptian kings of the 11th and 12th Dynasties. It contains the essential elements of a small garden from that period: walls to enclose, decorative palm trunks that support the porch roof for shade, edible red fruit on trees believed to be figs, and a central pond – here, copper-lined. It represents another way to take earthly possessions into the afterlife, to be enjoyed as they had been in life.

Architects and landscape designers continue to make models of projects and use them to explain designs to their clients.

GARDENS OF THE WORLD WITH AUDREY HEPBURN (1993), TV SERIES
Gardens on Television

A still from the television series Gardens of the World with Audrey Hepburn. *The first episode aired the day after her death, on 21st January 1993.*

'*To plant a garden is to believe in tomorrow.*'

AUDREY HEPBURN

As presenter of this well-received series created in the 1990s, Audrey Hepburn guided viewers through visits to the world's finest gardens. She was joined by noted garden experts for each of the eight episodes, including Penelope Hobhouse, John Brookes and Graham Stuart Thomas. Hepburn won an Emmy for 'Outstanding Individual Achievement, Informational Programming', awarded posthumously. She died on 20th January 1993.

Hepburn was known for her lifelong commitment to humanitarian work and was a goodwill ambassador for UNICEF. She donated her fee for this series to the charity.

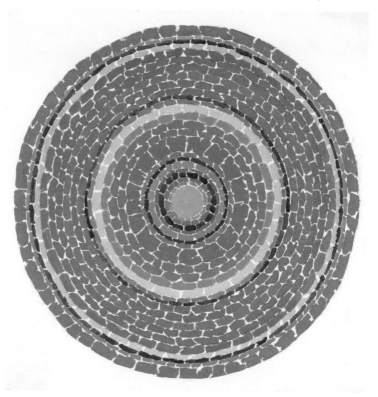

SPRINGTIME IN WASHINGTON (1971), ALMA WOODSEY THOMAS
An Abstract Garden

This painting of her garden shows Thomas's style, which has been described as reflecting Byzantine mosaic and pointillist techniques.

Washington DC-based African-American artist Alma Woodsey Thomas had retired from her career as a high school art teacher when she painted this picture. Her studio was her kitchen; her garden and nature inspired her work.

Thomas adopted an abstract style later in life and was 75 when she had her first exhibition of abstract work at Howard University in 1966. She was a role model for young Black Americans: she was the first African-American woman to have a solo exhibition at Whitney Museum of American Art, New York City, and exhibited paintings at the White House on three occasions. The third Monday of January is celebrated as Martin Luther King Day in the USA. It celebrates and honours the social rights and economic improvements for African Americans in the 20th century.

CHIHULY GARDEN AND GLASS, SEATTLE, USA
A Glass Garden

The red and yellow sculpture to the right of this picture is called 'The Sun', and was created by Dale Chihuly.

The intricate, colourful work of renowned American glassmaker Dale Chihuly has been exhibited in botanical gardens across the world. But at the museum that bears his name, he worked with a landscape designer to create a garden that showcases his creations. Displaying delicate glass in an outdoor space subject to seasonal weather changes seems an unlikely combination. But plants and glass artworks interact to make this a unique experience for visitors.

The garden's apt centrepiece is a 12-m (40-ft) glasshouse that embodies Chihuly's appreciation of conservatories. One of his largest sculptures is suspended overhead, an intricate garland of many different organic floral shapes in shades of red, orange, amber and yellow. It resembles a giant swag of nasturtiums captured in perpetual bloom.

VILLA NOAILLES, HYÈRES, FRANCE
A Cubist Garden

This triangular-shaped garden has a grid of beds and white walls.

Viewed from above, this angular garden resembles the prow of a ship. It was commissioned by the owners Viscount and Viscountess de Noailles after they saw Armenian designer Gabriel Guevrékian's show garden at the 1925 Paris Exposition, a very influential art and design exhibition.

The Cubist garden complements the modernist house, and its geometric design still looks contemporary today. Moving around the garden changes the viewer's perception of space and shapes. Although it has been restored, it remains faithful to the original concept, a rare survivor of the modernist garden movement in France.

CHARTWELL, WESTERHAM, KENT, ENGLAND
Sir Winston's Wall

A photograph
from 1950
showing Winston
Churchill
building a brick
wall in his garden
at Chartwell.

'A day away from Chartwell is a day wasted.'

SIR WINSTON CHURCHILL

Winston Churchill bought Chartwell in 1922 for its fine view. When he was re-elected as an MP in 1924, the house's location became convenient as it is within 40km (25 mi) of the House of Commons. Churchill loved the garden at Chartwell and was a keen bricklayer.

The Walled Garden was created from the mid-1920s onwards. A wall-mounted plaque acknowledges Churchill's role in building the walls: 'The greater part of this wall was built between the years 1925 & 1932 by Winston with his own hands.'

Among other changes made after 1945, the Golden Rose Garden was created in 1958, a gift from Winston and Clementine's children to mark their golden wedding anniversary. Churchill died on this day in 1965.

GLEN GRANT DISTILLERY GARDEN, ROTHES, NEAR ELGIN, SCOTLAND
The Whisky Garden

The Dram Pavilion in the gardens of Glen Grant Distillery. Not pictured: the whisky safe!

Taking a dram of whisky on Burns Night, the 25th January, is one of the traditions involved in celebrating the birth of Robert Burns. Major James Grant established extensive Victorian gardens around his distillery in 1886. This Dram Pavilion is a notable feature placed in the garden by Grant so that his guests could relax and enjoy the product of his distillery. The heather-thatched wooden building has a whisky safe inside. Higher up the steep-sided gorge is a smaller Dram Hut complete with another whisky safe.

Grant's interest in gardens is reflected in the planting. Paths wind through woodlands with many species of rhododendron, and a mature orchard. At its height, 11 gardeners were employed here. It took three years of research and work to reinstate the gardens after their decline. The Dram Pavilion was replaced on the evidence of old photographs.

THE AUSTRALIAN GARDEN, ROYAL BOTANIC GARDENS, CRANBORNE, MELBOURNE, AUSTRALIA
A Symbolic Garden

From above, the shape of the garden looks loosely like the shape of the country. Australia Day is celebrated on the 26th January.

It is hard to believe that the centre of this garden was once a quarry. This modern botanical garden tells a story rather than simply presents plant collections. Its layout traces the essential element of water throughout Australia and how different levels of it affect native vegetation. The planting shows the range of Australia's indigenous flora, encourages sustainability and emphasizes the importance of connection between people and landscapes.

THE GARDEN OF EXILE, JEWISH MUSEUM, BERLIN, GERMANY
A Memorial Garden

Angular and tilted containers provoke a sense of unease and constrain tree foliage.

This garden is defined by Polish-American architect Daniel Libeskind's 'Between the Lines' design for the building, which creates integral outside spaces. Accessed through a narrow, angular Axis of Exile, the garden was designed to create a sense of disorientation with feelings of uncertainty. Narrow paths traverse sloping ground through a grid of 49 tall concrete square tubes; 48 are filled with soil from Berlin and the central final one with soil from Jerusalem. All are planted with Russian olives (*Elaeagnus angustifolia*) that symbolize hope, but plant foliage is beyond reach. Libeskind wanted the sensation of being in this garden to embody the experience of the thousands of émigrés forced to leave their countries.

International Holocaust Memorial Day takes place each year on 27th January.

VILLA VIGNAMAGGIO, GREVE, ITALY
Much Ado About Nothing

Many successful garden designs combine concealed spaces with open areas, to increase privacy and add a sense of mystery. Villa Vignamaggio was the location for the 1993 film version of *Much Ado About Nothing*, directed by Kenneth Branagh.

The garden is central to Shakespeare's comedy *Much Ado About Nothing* (c.1599). Scene I is set in a garden belonging to Leonato, Duke of Messina. Its orchard is a place for overhearing confidences that facilitates the main plot to deceive in true and false love matches. Leonato's daughter Hero instructs her lady-in-waiting Margaret to persuade her cousin Beatrice to linger in a shaded place so that she can be tricked into believing Benedick is in love with her. It is the first of the play's series of deceptions, the use of openness and concealment, manipulation and loss of control.

Hero: *And bid her steal into the pleached bower,*
Where honeysuckles ripen'd by the sun,
Forbid the sun to enter, like favourites
Made proud by princes, that advance their pride
Against that power that bred it: there will she hide her,
To listen our purpose.

GARDEN LANDSCAPE (1905–15), LOUIS COMFORT TIFFANY
A Jewel-Like Garden

Garden Landscape represents a permanently shimmering garden view, with everlasting vibrant colours.

This beautiful mosaic may have been a study for a larger commission. Louis Comfort Tiffany was well known for highly decorative glass wares, stained-glass windows and mosaics – these last two mainly seen in churches. This serene garden scene is approximately 2.7 x 2.9m (9 x 9½ft) and used to grace the showroom of the Tiffany store in New York City, until the contents were auctioned in 1938. Tiffany's mosaic techniques were inspired by Byzantine examples seen on his travels; the frame around the scene references this inspiration. Tiffany experimented with iridescent glass and transparent tesserae backed with metal leaf, which gives this garden a jewel-like shimmer. It is in the collection of the Metropolitan Museum of Art, New York City.

EDEN PROJECT, CORNWALL, ENGLAND
The Garden of Eden

Some may argue that huge biomes sited in a disused Cornish china clay pit are not a garden in the traditional sense. But this project's main inspiration was to create a unique space where nature, plants and people's relationship with them is the focus. The Eden Project opened in 2001, and today it sits at the centre of a movement with a global mission. One biome has humid rainforest conditions with a waterfall feeding a watercourse that winds through exotic plants from the rainforest areas of the world. A slightly smaller biome is filled with plants from regions with a Mediterranean climate – including South Africa, Western Australia and California. Outdoor gardens surround the huge, high-tech conservatory biomes. It is an interesting garden to visit at any time of year, but a cold day at the end of January heightens the experience.

GARDENING LEAVE
Gardening from Home

Above: Old gardening boots make great plant pots in their retirement.

Opposite: Decking steps and walkways take visitors through Eden's canopy of lush plants.

For the gardener, the prospect of 'gardening leave' sounds idyllic. Exact details vary, but it may have little to do with taking time off to tend your garden. In the UK, a basic definition of the term is when an employer asks you not to come into work during your notice period, or to work at home or another location after handing in notice. You are contractually retained by your employer and still paid, but required to stay away from the workplace, and usually not to complete any work, or communicate with colleagues and employer's clients. Some sources place the term's origins in the Civil Service, and it was used in an episode of the 1980s, BBC political satire sitcom *Yes, Prime Minister*. Unlike for any keen gardener, in that instance, 'gardening leave' had negative overtones.

'BLOOMSBURY GARDEN', TIMOROUS BEASTIES
A Garden Pattern

This provocative design studio gives a new twist to a classical-looking pattern that is bursting with nature. Trailing stems echo past designs, including those of Morris & Co. Interwoven florals and fruits references interior designs of the Bloomsbury artists in bright shades. Flowers and fruits from different seasons are captured peaking together – violets, roses, clematis, roses, grapes, raspberries and pomegranates, interspersed with butterflies – creating a perpetually blooming garden.

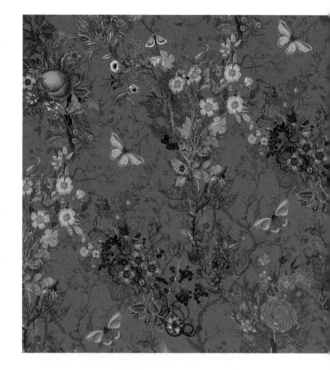

THE HAPPY GARDEN (1912), MARY ANSELL
In the Night Garden

The Happy Garden is a memoir about a garden, its atmosphere at different times of day and year, and the many joyful things a garden can bring to a life. In the book, author Mary Ansell describes memories of and feelings inspired by her garden at Black Lake Cottage, a weekend retreat and holiday home she shared with her husband, J. M. Barrie (see page 359). It was written after their divorce.

'THE GARDEN' (1938), ERIC RAVILIOUS
The Ceramic Garden

Above: Garden scenes are the reward for clearing one's plate!

Opposite top: Timorous Beasties 'Bloomsbury Garden' in teal in wallpaper and fabric

Opposite bottom: This frontispiece illustration of *The Happy Garden* is by Charles Dawson.

Eric Ravilious was an artist, designer, book illustrator and wood-engraver who worked in England between the wars. 'The Garden' was one of a series of commissions he produced for ceramics manufacturer Wedgwood in the 1930s. It shows how he applied modern design to the traditional production of high-quality tableware.

Although the design of these garden scenes was completed in 1938, production was interrupted by the Second World War. Ravilious died on active duty as a war artist in 1942 at the age of just 39. Many of his designs for Wedgwood did not enter full production until after his death.

GARDEN OF COSMIC SPECULATION, PORTRACK, DUMFRIES, SCOTLAND
Snake in Grass

A view of the Snake Mound's grass terraced landform curving around dark pools of water.

The landforms in this garden, completed in 2003, began with excavations to make a swimming pool at the home of Charles Jencks and his wife Maggie Keswick. Architect Jencks went on to re-design the whole garden into what he termed a 'landscape of waves' that explore a relationship with nature. This view of the Snake Mound shows the sculptural earthworks around organically-shaped water, one of the most famous elements in this garden. Other areas were inspired by DNA, the six senses, and theories on the creation of the universe. Classical elements of ground shaping were developed into a new approach to landscape garden making. Jencks died in 2021 at the age of 80.

APPLE PARK, CORPORATE HEADQUARTERS OF APPLE INC., CUPERTINO, CALIFORNIA, USA
The Corporate Garden

Trees at Apple Park include apples, apricots, cherries, pears and plums – referencing the history of this area as a centre of fruit production.

This garden fills the central space created by the massive circular building that is the corporate headquarters of Apple Inc. Co-founder Steve Jobs wanted the company campus to look more like a natural landscape than a commercial business site. Planning this headquarters was one of the last projects he oversaw, although sadly work did not start until several years after his death.

Renowned American landscape architect Laurie Olin was commissioned to design a masterplan; its subtle changes of topography and naturalistic planting brings a human scale to the space. The landscape is designed to be used, with winding pathways for walking, cycling or jogging. Planting is drought-resistant and is mostly native to the area, but includes non-native species better able to survive hotter summers, cooler winters and wetter storm conditions. Over 8,000 trees were planted, including productive orchards.

45

ST. ANNE'S COURT, CHERTSEY, SURREY, ENGLAND
A 20th-Century Garden

Lawns lead into wide, concrete steps that are set into the slope. The functional retaining wall combines a series of rectangular raised beds that are planted very simply.

Canadian landscape architect Christopher Tunnard moved to England to complete his studies in architecture and planning. His influential book *Gardens in the Modern Landscape* is a collection of articles first published by *The Architectural Review* between 1937 and 1938. Tunnard outlines the history of the garden, putting it in the context of landscape and life, and then explores how modern architecture and towns might influence garden and landscape design.

This house, originally called St. Anne's Hill, was designed by architect Raymond McGrath and is set in the remains of an 18th-century landscape. It was built for Tunnard, and his design for the garden reflects the approach set out in his book. Around the house, the garden is architectural and modernist, with a distinctive long concrete beam stretching out from the building and glass-walled rooms leading onto the terrace.

78 BANBURY ROAD, OXFORD, ENGLAND
Dr. James Murray's Scriptorium

Murray at his desk in the Scriptorium. Unseen is the team of lexicographers who worked with him there for many years. Murray sent so many letters to contributors all over the world that the Post Office installed a pillar box outside his house, which remains to this day.

Garden: *An enclosed piece of ground devoted to the cultivation of flowers, fruit, or vegetables.*

OXFORD ENGLISH DICTIONARY

Born on this day in 1837, Dr. James Murray went on to become principal editor of *A New English Dictionary on Historical Principles*, which later became the *Oxford English Dictionary*. When he built the iron shed – rather grandly known as the Scriptorium – in his garden in 1884, he was five years into the project that was forecast to take ten years to complete.

Giving a metal garden building a classical name matches the scale and importance of the task. Murray started his editorship while still teaching at Mill Hill School in London and had built an earlier version. The larger Oxford Scriptorium had custom-built pigeonholes sized to fit the slips of paper that were used to trace the origins, principles and use of words.

GARDENS FOR MENTAL AND PHYSICAL HEALTH
The Well-Minded Garden

Gardens can cultivate a sense of peace and well-being at any time of year, as seen in The Barn, Tom and Sue Stuart-Smith's garden. For another view of this garden, see page 175.

That gardens are good for mental health and a sense of well-being has been known for centuries. A winter garden book by French author Jean Franeau, *Jardin d'hyver ou cabinet des fleurs*, which was designed to keep the spirits lifted through darker months, was published in 1616. Fast-forward to recent times, and many studies have shown the measurable neurological benefits of simply looking at plants, and that hospital inpatients heal faster when looking at green spaces.

Gardening as a form of physical exercise is also good for you, relieving stress and promoting a feeling of well-being. In *The Well Gardened Mind – Rediscovering Nature in the Modern World* (2020), renowned psychiatrist, psychotherapist and gardener Sue Stuart-Smith looks at the therapeutic benefits of gardens and gardening. Recently, she and her husband Tom have incorporated these themes into their own garden and also created the Serge Hill Community Project in their orchard, which provides space for community allotments.

WADDESDON MANOR, BUCKINGHAMSHIRE, ENGLAND
A Tapestry of Bulbs and Flowers

Waddesdon's mounded formal borders make colourful garden highlights that are revitalized twice a year.

Between 1874 and 1879, Baron Ferdinand de Rothschild had these formal gardens around his new French style château designed by his landscape designer Elie Lainé, to display his collection of Italian, French and Dutch statues. At the height of this fashion, the number of bedding plants used was a measure of wealth. Waddesdon's curving formal beds are mounded, which adds height and depth to colour effects. Spring-flowering plants interspersed with bulbs are planted in October, for colour the following year. In May, beds are replanted with summer-flowering plants for colour throughout the following months. Today, Waddesdon uses high-tech methods to design these displays. Real carpets or tapestries from the house are scanned, pixillated and turned into a planting plan, enabling colour matching and growing the right numbers of the different types of plants. Time-lapse sequences in online virtual garden tours show all the skills behind this traditional way of filling borders with seasonal colour.

THE GARDEN OF EDEN
The First Garden

The Garden of Eden is traditionally placed in Mesopotamia, the area of land in between the Tigris and Euphrates rivers in the Middle East. The wetter northern area of the area known as the Fertile Crescent would support a fruiting apple tree. The concept of a first paradise garden is interwoven in different cultures, and has been depicted in artworks and written about throughout history.

Adam, the first man, was charged with looking after a fertile, fragrant paradise that would provide food without work. After the Fall, he and Eve were sent out of the garden, where Adam was told he would now have to work to provide food – 'till the ground' (Genesis, Chapter 3, Verse 23).

'FLOWER GARDEN' (1879), WILLIAM MORRIS
A Fabric Garden

Above: 'Flower Garden' is one of over 50 botanical wallpaper designs by William Morris.

Opposite: This 12th-century stained-glass window at Canterbury Cathedral shows Adam 'delving' with a rudimentary spade. It is unusual to see him at work.

William Morris described this fabric design as 'looking beautiful, like a flower garden'. His fabric designs were produced using traditional, pre-industrial methods. This flower garden is a handloom jacquard of silk and wool and was used for a number of commissions. Morris's fabric designs were used for curtains and drapes that were wall hung, in a way similar to tapestries in earlier times. A return to medieval-style furnishings was very much part of Morris's design ethos: an everlasting flower garden to be appreciated all year long.

YI-HE-YUAN (GARDEN OF PRESERVING HARMONY), BEIJING, CHINA
The Summer Palace Garden

Each beam of the Long Corridor is painted with a scene from Chinese folk tales and classical stories. Chinese New Year is celebrated between 21st January and 20th February every year.

The garden of the Summer Palace is not far from Beijing's Forbidden City. At its heart is the *Kunming Hu* – Vast Bright Lake – which was created from a former stream. Construction took place in the 18th century and early 19th century. It was started by Emperor Qianlong, who was an expert on making gardens according to the principles of Chinese landscape design, which balances natural features with those built by people.

After the garden was largely destroyed by wars in the 1850s and 1860s, it was rebuilt by the Emperor Guangxu for use by Dowager Empress Cixi and she gave the garden the name it is known by today. Surviving more damage and periods of restoration, it has been a public park since 1924. In a garden made on such a breathtaking scale as this, exceptional features include the Seventeen Arched Bridge linking islands in the lake and the Long Corridor, a covered walkway stretching 700 m (2,300 ft).

VIEW FROM THE TERRACE OF A VILLA AT NITON, ISLE OF WIGHT, FROM SKETCHES BY A LADY (1826), J. M. W. TURNER
Italian Garden, English View

The painting shows the view across private grounds, down to a natural beach. The scenery of the Isle of Wight was a constant source of inspiration for Turner.

This garden painting by J. M. W. Turner is a rare collaboration with the villa's owner, Lady Julia Gordon, who had been his pupil in 1797, and also studied with other respected artists. Turner gave it the title *View from the Terrace of a Villa at Niton, Isle of Wight, from Sketches by a Lady* when it was exhibited at the Royal Academy in 1826.

The painting shows the new fashion for Italian-style gardens. The terrace helps frame the view of the English Channel, just east of the most southerly point of the Isle of Wight. The villa was usually portrayed from this seaward side, as it has cliffs looming behind. This terraced garden and its view were famous and remained fine enough to warrant a visit by Queen Victoria on 13th February 1867. Unfortunately, however, it was a foggy day so she missed this fine view.

TAJ MAHAL, AGRA, INDIA
Garden as a Love Story

Above: The ultimate love-story garden.

Opposite top: This photograph of Miller's writing studio was taken by his wife Inge Morath in 1963.

Opposite bottom: Bacon's notion of perpetual spring with year-round colour is an ideal that endures to this day.

Created by Shah Jahan, it took over 20 years to create the world-famous marble mausoleum and its garden setting for his most beloved wife Mumtaz Mahal. The scale of the *chahar bagh* four-quartered garden layout derives from the size of the building and its architectural features; the long canal is centred on the main archway. Sunlight plays a dramatic role in this garden, as it alters the building's colour through the day – from the milky opalescence of daybreak to the golden tones of sunset.

ARTHUR MILLER'S WRITING STUDIO, ROXBURY, CONNECTICUT, USA
A Private Space to Create

Arthur Miller wrote in this small writing studio for almost 50 years. This was the second one he built on the same road in rural Connecticut, after moving house in 1958. The American playwright repurposed a wooden door into his first desk for this cabin. He wrote here in the mornings and worked on his land or in his carpentry workshop in the afternoons. This studio also held the archive of his essential writing, from college letters sent home to family in the 1930s, to famous plays and his journals.

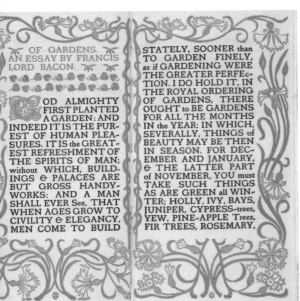

OF GARDENS (1625), FRANCIS BACON
A Perpetual Spring

In his essay *Of Gardens*, Lord Chancellor, philosopher, scientist and gardener Francis Bacon describes ordering his ideal garden so that different areas have plants that give interest year-round. Bacon's garden calendar lists the months and plants to include, suited to the climate in the gardens of London. He argues that this ensures a state of *Ver perpetuum* – perpetual life – or spring.

THE HANGING GARDENS OF BABYLON
Garden Wonder of the Ancient World

The hand-painted 19th-century woodcut shows a Victorian imagining of the Hanging Gardens.

The Hanging Gardens of Babylon were one of the Seven Wonders of the Ancient World. Created by King Nebuchadnezzar II in the 6th century BCE for his wife, who was homesick for the lush hills of her native Persia (modern-day Iran), the gardens were well documented by ancient scholars and historians as a feat of extraordinary engineering and planting skills. Destroyed by earthquakes, no trace of them has been found, but research has discovered an ancient site of similar scale hundreds of miles away in Nineveh, on the Tigris River, near Mosul in modern-day Iraq.

Many people are nostalgic for the plants of the country of their birth and gardens of their youth, which can inspire their gardening.

LETCHWORTH GARDEN CITY, HERTFORDSHIRE, ENGLAND
A Garden City

The front gardens of the Arts and Crafts houses in Letchworth Garden City.

Social reformer Ebenezer Howard outlined his ideas to solve the problems of urban poverty and overcrowded squalid city slums in *Tomorrow: A Real Path to Social Reform* (1898). Building a new type of town – a garden city – was central to his plan. This would combine the best aspects of town and country in a planned community, with rents from businesses, industries, shops and surrounding farms reinvested locally.

Founded in 1903, Letchworth Garden City became the world's first garden city, laid out with a garden for every home and public green spaces that bring the countryside into the town.

PROSPECT COTTAGE, DEREK JARMAN'S GARDEN, DUNGENESS, KENT, ENGLAND
A Driftwood and Flint Garden

Colourful plants, simple stone patterns and considered placement of driftwood anchor the garden of Prospect Cottage into the surrounding stark landscape of Dungeness.

Derek Jarman bought Prospect Cottage in 1986 and created this garden in under ten years. The vast shingle landscape surrounding it has a surreal quality enhanced by the mass of the Dungeness nuclear power station. But this stretch of coastline is home to a wealth of native plant species, insects and wildlife.

Jarman anchored his vision of a paradise garden by defining a series of stone circles from flints and shells. Pieces of driftwood and found objects punctuate the garden. Planting is spare yet surprisingly colourful. An influential space, Jarman called it his 'dragon-toothed' garden, its purpose to defend his house. Gardening gave him solace after his HIV diagnosis.

Following his death on this day in 1994, the future of his legacy has recently been secured by a major Art Fund purchase of the cottage and garden in their entirety.

MAGGIE'S CENTRES, UK
Gardens of Care

The garden at Maggie's, Southampton. This garden was designed by Chelsea Gold Medal winner Sarah Price.

The Maggie Keswick Jencks Cancer Caring Centres Trust, or simply Maggie's, is a charity providing free cancer support and information across the UK.

Founder Maggie Keswick Jencks based a new type of cancer care on her own experience of having the illness. A writer and gardener, she was diagnosed with breast cancer at the age of 47, and it returned five years later in 1993. Maggie devised a masterplan for the centres, together with her husband, American cultural theorist and landscape designer Charles Jencks. They are spaces where people can come together outside hospitals but close to them. Maggie Keswick Jencks believed in the power of beautifully designed buildings to uplift people and the importance of gardens as calm spaces – the centres are generally set in beautiful gardens. Sadly, she died before the first Maggie's Centre opened at Western General Hospital, Edinburgh in 1996.

THE PRINCESS MEETS A TALKING FROG IN HER GARDEN (C.1874), WALTER CRANE
A Fairy Tale Garden

This illustration is from the first edition of Walter Crane's book The Frog Prince.

In the famous Brothers Grimm fairy tale, a beautiful young princess meets a frog in the castle garden after she has dropped her favourite golden ball into a pool. This illustration by Walter Crane captures the moment in a version of *The Frog Prince* produced in 1874.

Children's books were transformed by Crane's distinctive illustrations. This was in a 'toy' book series for very young children, but while his strong Arts and Crafts style makes no concessions to youth, its vivid details are inspiring for all ages. Crane was a friend of William Morris and shared his artistic beliefs.

MOUNT VERNON, VIRGINIA, USA
An American Garden

George Washington was born on the 22nd February, 1732. At Mount Vernon, the third week of February is full of family events to mark the occasion.

First president of the USA, George Washington was a gardener and wrote extensively on gardening in his diaries. His formal design for Mount Vernon's upper garden showcased his particular interest in fruit trees and vegetables for household use.

The kitchen garden is functional and beautiful: ornamental shrubs and flowering plants surround the box-edged beds. Washington planned the brick greenhouse or hothouse as a focal point. He researched the construction of its heated floor. Thick brick walls insulate against winter cold, large south-facing windows can be opened from the top or bottom. Citrus fruit were grown for culinary use, and imported tender plants were also displayed.

There were few heated greenhouses in North America when this one was created in 1784. Low side wings were added later to provide housing for the enslaved people who worked at Mount Vernon.

ROCK GARDEN OF CHANDIGARH, INDIA
A Sculpture Garden

A brightly coloured group of sculpted forms are just one of the many curious features in Nek Chand's fantastic creation.

This intriguing rock garden is better described as a sculpture garden. Created by Nek Chand, a government official, it began in 1957 as a hobby on a canyon site near his home in Chandigarh, using stones and waste materials collected in the course of his work. Remarkably, the large groups of curious statues and animal figures that populate the garden were kept a secret from his employers for years. But when word got out, support for Chand's project from the community was so strong that his employers decided to allocate the necessary labour and budget to help him complete the garden.

Today, his unique garden made from all types of waste materials covers 20ha (50 ac) and is visited by thousands of people every day.

GARDENING WITHOUT WORK (1961), RUTH STOUT
The No-Work Garden

The original
front cover of
*Gardening Without
Work* shows Stout
relaxing in a
wheelbarrow!

American author and gardener Ruth Stout was well known for her series of 'No Work' gardening books. She first adopted a different approach to gardening in the 1920s and became known as the 'Mulch Queen'; her premise was that being kinder to the Earth was also being kinder to yourself.

Her books were based on personal experience and her garden showed the results. Stout's top layer of mulch was hay or straw, which she bought in. Many of her methods are more widespread today: no digging; the importance of composting; applying a mulch to conserve and boost nutrients and reduce watering; and recycling as much as possible. In short, working with nature rather than against it.

THE HANGING GARDENS OF MARQUEYSSAC, SARLAT, PÉRIGORD, FRANCE
Julien's Labyrinth

Interlocking trimmed box plants pattern the terraces with organic sculptural forms.

This garden of pure theatre is suspended from a rocky outcrop above the Dordogne river. It was created in the 19th century by retired soldier Julien de Cérval when he inherited the château. He planted 150,000 specimens of common box (*Buxus sempervirens*) throughout the site and clipped them in elaborately designed parterres and topiary shapes. After a period of neglect, 3,500 new box plants were added to the 100-year-old originals during the restoration in 1996. Paths radiate from the central viewpoint and meander through the garden. Black-as-night tunnels and shady corners add to the romantic atmosphere. Box plants are clipped to perfection into giant jigsaws of green sculptural shapes. It is an evergreen garden in every sense.

CARL LINNAEUS HOME AND GARDEN, UPPSALA, SWEDEN
An Ordered Garden

Buildings housing Carl Linnaeus's extensive natural history collections. Many important visitors came here to meet the eminent man.

'If you do not know the names of things, the knowledge of them is lost too.'
CARL LINNAEUS

In 1753, Swedish scientist Carl Linnaeus published the two-word binomial (or binominal) Latin plant-naming system that changed the way plants are accurately identified. It was also adopted for identifying animals, in a way that was consistent in all countries, and was crucial in the development of scientific knowledge and its international communication. His system is still used today.

Linnaeus's own garden was at Hammarby, his country farm, a summer family retreat away from urban Uppsala where he was a professor at the university. He grew plants to increase his knowledge of all aspects of their cultivation. It was effectively an outdoor laboratory for his work.

LINGERING GARDEN, SUZHOU, JIANGSU, CHINA
A Ming Dynasty Garden

This moon gate invites visitors to pass from one part of Lingering Garden to another.

The aptly named Lingering Garden is a Ming dynasty masterpiece originally conceived and built by Xu Tashi in the 16th century. From a simple entrance, a plain courtyard opens into a garden vision of a 'natural' landscape. A twisting route of paths through planting and around buildings makes the garden appear much larger than its actual size.

A pebble mosaic paved path leads through a moon gate to The Small Garden of Stone Forest. Curious shaped stones are one of the garden's most famous features. They were collected from the large freshwater Lake Tai, or Taihu, whose waters have eroded them into sculptural forms. The largest of these stones, the Cloud Capped Peak, stands at over 6 m (21 ft) tall.

Expanded in the early 19th century and restored twice after damage, the garden retains the original concept. It's definitely a garden to linger in.

TŌFUKU-JI, KYOTO, JAPAN
20th-Century Zen

This is a garden of carefully chosen and positioned rocks and raked gravel – there are no plants to distract the mind within this space.

Tōfuku-ji is one of the five great Zen temples in Kyoto. In 1939, the abbot commissioned landscape architect Mirei Shigemori to design the South Garden. Relatively unknown at the time, Shigemori had immersed himself in the history, philosophy and theory of Japanese garden design. This garden, with its raked gravel abstract patterns, brings the historic art of Japanese garden design into the 20th century without losing its most important traditions.

GOOD GRIEF! GARDENING IS HARD WORK! (1999), CHARLES M. SCHULZ
Garden Mischief

Snoopy is often
seen in reclining
mode in a garden,
either on the roof
of his kennel or
more comfortably
as shown.

Not everyone finds gardening a pleasurable activity. In the story in this book of the popular cartoon characters, Lucy enlists 'help' to get her garden ready for vegetable growing. But what she really wants is someone else to do all the hard work under her watchful eye. Snoopy becomes a hired hand by claiming gardening experience he does not have, with inevitable consequences.

Being clear about what you are really asking for help with in your garden and not making false claims of experience are important things to take away from this lighthearted gardening story!

PLAS BRONDANW, GWYNEDD, WALES
Sir Clough Williams-Ellis's Garden

A dusting of snow on hedge tops and topiary reflects the white topping on Eryi on this St. David's Day.

Welsh architect Sir Clough Williams-Ellis created his garden throughout his life. The architect is more famous for designing the Italianate fantasy village, Portmeirion, which is close by (see page 104).

Set within a National Park, the garden at Plas Brondanw is something of a secret place. Inspired by Italian Renaissance gardens, the sloping site is divided into compartments by yew hedges, topiary shapes and terraces, with stone retaining walls. Unusual sculptures and items of architectural salvage are well placed. But overall, this garden is all about the view of the dramatic landscape of Eryri (Snowdonia) beyond.

KIRSTENBOSCH NATIONAL BOTANIC GARDEN, CAPETOWN, SOUTH AFRICA
A Magnificent Botanic Garden

Kirstenbosch is one of the world's great botanic gardens. The site, with its superb backdrop of Table Mountain, was bought by Cecil Rhodes and he planted the Camphor Avenue and nearby Moreton Bay Figs in 1898 – some still survive. The land was bequeathed to the government on his death in 1902.

Harold Pearson was Professor of Botany at the South African College. Seeing the need for a botanic garden in Capetown, this garden was established in 1913 with Pearson as its director.

Kirstenbosch shows the huge diversity of native South African plants on what was once neglected farmland. For the first 50 years, all work was done by hand, the terrain making it more challenging. Pearson died in 1916 and is buried in the garden. His successor Robert Compton and first curator J. W. Matthews did an enormous amount to develop the beautiful garden seen today.

SÍTIO ROBERTO BURLE MARX, RIO DE JANEIRO, BRAZIL
From Berlin to Brazil

Above: Burle Marx was renowned for his bold use of plants and used his garden as a testing ground.

Opposite: This garden is often listed as one of the seven most magnificent botanical gardens in the world.

This lush garden was a landscape laboratory where its creator Roberto Burle Marx experimented with native plants. The famous landscape designer, gardener, artist and singer was also an environmentalist, committed to preserving Brazil's native flora. But he only discovered his country's native plants while studying opera in Berlin, where he saw them growing in glasshouses at the Berlin-Dahlem Botanical Garden and Botanical Museum and fell in love with them. This was life-changing; on his return to Brazil, he became a landscape designer. His designs are like modern abstract paintings with organic ground shapes filled with big, bold blocks of plants or pools of water. Burle Marx introduced modern gardens to South America and influenced designers in North America and Europe.

CHÂTEAU DE VERSAILLES, FRANCE
The Garden of the Sun King

High-
maintenance
garden formality
on a grand
scale was not a
problem for the
Sun King.

This garden is a huge statement, a display of King Louis XIV's power over both nature and politics. It took 40 years to complete the monumental project and Louis wanted to review each part personally.

Today, the garden is about half the size it was when first created. Despite the large scale, its designer André Le Nôtre used symmetry and geometry to create smaller, more intimate areas, and some of these hold surprises. To maintain the design, the garden has been replanted approximately every 100 years. A devastating storm in December 1999 required more extensive renovation, but the gardens today appear as they would have looked to Louis XIV, the Sun King, himself.

AMBER FORT GARDEN, AMER, JAIPUR, INDIA
Floating Carpet Garden

This is one
of a series of
manicured
gardens found
in the superb
architecture of
the Amber Fort.

The Kesar Kyari (Saffron Garden) is sited on a large platform built on top of a rock that rises out of the Maota Lake. Designed to be viewed from above by the women of the palace harem, it appears like a giant floating carpet, its pattern of interlocking geometrically shaped flower beds defined by marble shows the traditions of both Islamic and Hindu symbolism. It is also known as the Maunbari Garden, as it is believed that the night-time view of it from the palace above was important, when the pattern of its pale marble flower beds would stand out in the darkness.

DEWSTOW GARDENS & GROTTOES, MONMOUTHSHIRE, WALES
An Underground Garden

When this garden was rediscovered in the late 20th century, the underground areas were remarkably intact.

A director of the Great Western Railway, known locally as Squire Oakley, Henry Oakley created this mysterious garden after he bought the Dewstow Estate in 1893. Cultivating ferns, tropical plants and flowers were his main horticultural interests. At ground level he created rock gardens, pools, water features and a stumpery, and he planted a mixture of trees, shrubs and herbaceous plants from around the world. Exotic tender plants filled large glasshouses.

But it is what he created underground that makes this garden unique: an extensive system of artificial rockwork – Pulhamite – comprising tunnels, grottoes and caverns filled with ferns and other shade-loving plants. After Oakley's death, this unusual underground network survived neglect and the construction of the nearby M4 motorway. When rediscovered, it required remarkably few repairs to present in the good condition seen today.

JARDIN MAJORELLE, MARRAKECH, MOROCCO
A Blue Garden

Bold colours on buildings and features are counterbalanced by strong architectural plant shapes at the Jardin Marjorelle.

This garden is a cool refuge from the Moroccan heat. It was created by French artist Jacques Majorelle, born on this day in 1886, at the villa he had built in 1923. Classic canals, fountains and pools are defined in an intense colour known as 'Majorelle blue'. It complements the flower and foliage colours of the surprisingly lush planting. Majorelle lived here until his divorce in the 1950s. Previously full of the artist's extraordinary plant collections, the garden went into decline until it was bought by fashion designer Yves Saint Laurent and his partner Pierre Bergé in 1980. Together they restored it to its original glory.

The house has a Berber Museum, and in 2017, an Yves Saint Laurent Museum opened nearby.

RYDER'S SEEDS, ST. ALBANS, HERTFORDSHIRE, ENGLAND
The Ryder Cup Garden

The red brick building next to the conservatory used to house the Ryder's Seeds offices. Buried in its foundations is a time capsule containing a packet of Ryder's Seeds, a seed catalogue and a history of the company.

Ryder's Seeds' success was based on a mail-order service with fast response times. Founded by Samuel Ryder in the 1890s, it became a public company in the early 1920s and soon employed 300 staff. This art deco exhibition hall conservatory on Holywell Hill in the centre of St. Albans was opened in 1930. Designed by Percy Blow, it showcased the company's products and demonstrated plant displays.

Ryder was active in the community and supported local charities. As president of the St. Albans Horticultural Society, he presented them with a silver cup to be awarded for gardening. Although the company and society no longer exist, the lesser-known Ryder Cup came into the care of Ayletts, a local nursery, whose allotment group award it as an annual prize – unlike the other Ryder Cup, which is biannual.

THE MASTER OF THE FISHING NETS GARDEN, SUZHOU, JIANGSU, CHINA
A Garden of Lyrical Names

Classical pavilions supported on piers or rocks appear to hover over the pool. Planting includes blossoming trees, evergreen shrubs, bamboo and lower growing ornamental grasses.

Suzhou is famed for its excellent classical gardens. The Master-of-the-Fishing-Nets-Garden is thought by some to be the finest, although it is one of the smaller ones. The first garden on this site was created in 1140, but had fallen into disrepair by the time it was acquired by Song Zongyuan in 1785. Song redesigned it quite extensively. A scholar's garden, named after the fisherman's hermitage, it displays the classical elements of Chinese garden design: a residential area, central main garden and inner garden – all linked by buildings and structures with proportions that match the site.

It's a garden full of descriptively named spaces and pavilions. Entry is through the residence into a central area called the Place for Gathering Breezes, with the Rosy Clouds Pool, surrounded at the sides by the Washing-My-Ribbon Pavilion and the Moon Comes with Breeze pavilion. Late Spring Cottage courtyard leads to the Peony Study.

THE GARTH, GLOUCESTER CATHEDRAL, GLOUCESTERSHIRE, ENGLAND
From Richard II to Harry Potter

Once a busy part of the monastery, this garden is a peaceful place of reflection.

Fans of the Harry Potter films will recognize the fine fan vaulting of the cloisters enclosing this garden, as Gloucester Cathedral was one of the locations used in the series. But this garden is less well known. The cloisters and garden or 'garth' were the heart of medieval monasteries, as this cathedral was originally. Unusually, these cloisters are located on the north side of the building (a church's cloisters are usually found on the south side).

In October 1378, the young Richard II held a meeting of Parliament in one of the rooms within the precinct. Attendant courtiers played boisterous games in this garden. The abbey chronicler recorded '... the green of the cloister was so flattened by wrestlings and ball games that it was hopeless to expect any grass to be left there.'

Now it is a place for quiet reflection, where visitors may also spot peregrine falcons flying around the tower.

THE GARDEN OF EARTHLY DELIGHTS (1490–1500), HIERONYMUS BOSCH
Godly and Godless Gardens

The Garden of Earthly Delights (oil on oak panel, 1490–1500), Hieronymus Bosch

This triptych was painted late in the career of Dutch artist Hieronymus Bosch and is his most complex work. While its title was bestowed in modern times, the painting represents the religious beliefs and morality of the time in which it was painted. It is a graphical depiction, designed to be read like a book in a time when many were unable to read. It shows the Creation, the earthly paradise of the Garden of Eden, the first temptation and the Fall. Surreal landscapes are underlined with fantastical beasts interwoven with a representation of the concept of sin, deception and false paradise through the pursuit of carnal pleasures. Damnation, Hell and punishments inflicted on various types of sinners are shown in the right-hand panel.

SEZINCOTE, GLOUCESTERSHIRE, ENGLAND
Indian Influence

Sezincote's
architecture and
Paradise Garden
belie its rural
Gloucestershire
setting.

It is surprising to find a Mughal-style house in the wooded hills of Gloucestershire. The house and garden buildings were designed in 1805 by Samuel Pepys Cockerell for his brother Sir Charles, who had spent time in India. Humphry Repton laid out the grounds, which include an Indian-style bridge and ornaments of Brahmin bulls.

This Paradise Garden was created in 1968. Inspired by a visit to India, Lady Kleinwort worked with Graham Stuart Thomas on the design. The *chahar bagh* is centred on the house, with the cross path linking to the conservatory pavilion entrance.

HERSCHEL MUSEUM OF ASTRONOMY, BATH, ENGLAND
A Garden of Discoveries

Herschel's home is now the Herschel Museum of Astronomy and the garden has been designed with planting typical of a Georgian townhouse.

'I have looked further into space than any human being did before me.'

WILLIAM HERSCHEL

On 13th March 1781, William Herschel discovered the seventh planet Uranus observing the skies from the garden of his house in Bath. Until then, the Earth's Solar System was thought to contain just six planets. Herschel used a telescope he designed and made himself.

German-born Herschel came to England as a musician and worked in Bath. Self-taught in mathematics and science, he became interested in astronomy. When he found the telescopes available to be of a poor quality, he taught himself how to make better instruments in his home – a risky process involving molten metal. His sister Caroline joined him in the UK and helped with his work. She was also an accomplished astronomer.

GEORGE EASTMAN MUSEUM (HOUSE), ROCHESTER, NEW YORK, USA
A Picture Perfect Garden

Above: Formal terraces near the house are camera-ready.

Opposite top: Naturalistic planting around waterfalls.

Opposite bottom: Vegetables, herbs and flowers combine well with ornamental planting.

George Eastman was a pioneer of popular photography and motion picture film. He made his fortune as founder of the Eastman Kodak Company, which made camera-owning and photography widely accessible.

Following his death on this day in 1932, the grand house he had built became a museum of photography. Opened in 1949, it is the world's oldest photography museum, housing a large collection of international material including many early, rare garden images.

Eastman's garden was designed by landscape architect Alling Stephen DeForest and combines flower-filled terraces, long pergolas and sunken pools. Restoration and ongoing maintenance have been aptly aided by the abundant photographic records of the garden – something all gardeners can copy.

AYRLIES GARDEN, WHITFORD, AUCKLAND, NEW ZEALAND
A Paradise Garden

This is one of New Zealand's finest gardens. Beverley and Malcom McConnell transformed dairy paddocks and fields purchased in 1964 into a magnificent series of garden rooms, each with its own distinctive character. Eclectic planting is made possible by mastery of the coastal climate and soil conditions. A series of water features make natural-looking backdrops to plants such as tree ferns, gunnera, magnolia, roses and exotic puya.

LE MANOIR AUX QUAT SAISONS, OXFORDSHIRE, ENGLAND
From Garden to Table

Raymond Blanc was one of the earliest chefs to make a garden to grow vegetables and herbs for his restaurant. Fresh produce is at its best when it has travelled the shortest possible distance and looks good in the ground of this *potager* or kitchen garden. Blanc is currently re-planting an orchard with old varieties of British and French apples.

POWERSCOURT GARDENS, ENNISKERRY, COUNTY WICKLOW, IRELAND
A Garden Terraced by Hand

Fountain, pool and the Wicklow Mountains make the perfect view from the great terrace and steps at Powerscourt on St. Patrick's Day.

How better to celebrate St. Patrick's Day than by enjoying the view from the top terrace at Powerscourt Gardens, looking over the Triton Pond to the distinctively shaped Sugarloaf Mountain. The garden as seen today is largely the design of architect Daniel Robertson; the terraces, expansive steps and formal areas were created in the mid-19th century. It is said that sculpting the great terraces took over 12 years with 100 workers using ordinary garden tools in an age before mechanized earthworks – an extraordinary feat. Other areas are planted with conifers and trees collected by Lord Powerscourt. It is a garden where control has been exerted over the natural landscape.

REPTON'S RED BOOKS
Gardens Revealed

A spread from
one of Repton's
Red Books. The
watercolour
scene shows
'before', and
lifting flaps reveal
the view 'after'
his proposals
have been
implemented.

Humphry Repton was the leading landscape designer of his time. After an unsuccessful career in business, his interest in botany spurred him to learn about landscape gardening for a change of career.

In making his designs, Repton not only took into account practical matters such as site topography, but also his clients' homes and how they lived. His famous Red Books are his legacy. The innovative bound volumes show his proposals in detailed form. Clients were presented with watercolour 'before' views, with sliding or lifting sections showing 'after' impressions of his completed designs. In effect, they are the virtual reality reveals of the late 18th and early 19th centuries.

HET LOO PALACE, APELDOORN, THE NETHERLANDS
The Garden of Perpetual Youth

These formal parterres are as crisply defined as a giant cross stitch sampler.

The existing gardens at Het Loo were improved after William and Mary were crowned King and Queen of England in 1689. Intricate box parterres and gravel-filled *parterres de broderie* were designed by Daniel Marot, a Huguenot who fled France in 1685. A *berceau* or arched trellis among tall hedges was specially designed to keep the sun off the Queen. All detail was later lost due to the preference for English landscape-style gardens in the 18th century.

Restored to its original design in the 1970s, this garden is now maintained precisely how it would have appeared c.1700 – in perpetual youth.

VILLA D'ESTE, TIVOLI, ITALY
Hydraulic Horticulture

Hydraulic engineering and the steep slope produces spectacular results as seen in the many water features at Villa d'Este.

One of the great Italian Renaissance gardens, this was built for Cardinal Ippolito d'Este, born on this day in 1479. The design is attributed to architect Pirro Ligorio, who was very influential in the garden design of the period.

The terraced steep slope is gradually revealed from the entrance, originally at the bottom, today from the top. Water is the main theme, used in many different features in feats of hydraulic engineering that are still operational today. There are no pumps – every fountain is gravity-fed. A hidden mechanism triggers the Owl fountain to soak unsuspecting visitors. The three-tiered Terrace of the Hundred Fountains is another well-known feature.

The ambitious cardinal never became pope, but his spectacular garden is an enduring legacy.

LES JARDINS D'ETRETAT, NORMANDY, FRANCE
The Garden of Emotions

Sculptural faces express a range of emotions as they appear to float on top of a textural surface of clipped common box.

The seven gardens that comprise Les Jardins d'Etretat were created by Russian designer Alexandre Grivko at his home Villa Roxelane on the Normandy coast. Since 2017, he has reimagined the steep clifftop site with beautiful Channel views, respecting its history and tricky slope but updating its concept. Planting is like living sculpture in this outdoor gallery of contemporary art, with a core permanent collection and annual displays. Jardin Émotions was inspired by the first French oyster farm, located in the sea at the foot of the cliff below and owned by Marie Antoinette. Clipped common box (*Buxus sempervirens*) represent the seafloor landscape and supports a collection of sculpted faces by Spanish artist Samuel Salcedo titled *Des Gouttes de Pluie*. These raindrops show a range of emotions that prompt different emotional responses to this garden.

PEARL FRYAR TOPIARY GARDEN, BISHOPVILLE, SOUTH CAROLINA, USA
A Gift to All

Access to this garden is free – a gift to all. In 2015, the Garden Conservancy acknowledged it as one of the 50 most notable gardens across the USA.

'It wasn't important to me to create a garden. I wanted to create a feeling, so that when you walk through here you feel different than when you came in.'

PEARL FRYAR

Pearl Fryar is a self-taught topiary artist and began making this garden in 1984 with plants that were salvaged from composting piles at local plant nurseries . Today, the 1.2-ha (3-ac) garden is home to a collection of hundreds of unique topiary shapes and 'junk art' sculptures.

Fryar was the first African-American man to win his neighbourhood's 'Yard of the Month' award. He is known for his kindness, dedication and positive thinking. A message carved into the ground and emphasized with red bedding plants is a year-round centrepiece not just for the festive period: 'LOVE PEACE and GOODWILL'.

GARDEN MUSEUM, LAMBETH, LONDON, ENGLAND
A History of Gardens

Engraved tombstones and fine planting reflect the history of the site of the Garden Museum.

This courtyard garden lies at the heart of the museum that tells the story of British gardens and gardening. It was originally established in 1976 in the deconsecrated church of St. Mary-at-Lambeth because its churchyard held the tombs of both John Tradescants, Elder and Younger. Father and son were renowned 16th- and 17th-century botanists and gardeners.

A modern extension was added to the building in 2014 and the garden redesigned by Dan Pearson. He drew inspiration from the plant-collecting journeys of both Tradescants and other renowned plant hunters up to the present day. This calm oasis of rare plants and architectural foliage is punctuated by the tombs of the Tradescants and William Bligh, Captain of HMS *Bounty* on its infamous voyage.

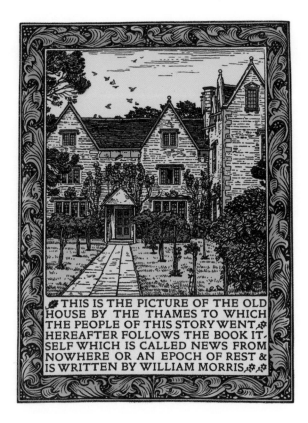

KELMSCOTT MANOR, KELMSCOTT, WEST OXFORDSHIRE, ENGLAND
News from Nowhere Garden

The title page of William Morris's book *News from Nowhere,* Kelmscott Press, (1892), shows the house and front garden, a view that he considered utopian.

William Morris admired the existing garden as much as historic Kelmscott Manor when he discovered it in 1871. The textile designer, writer, architectural conservator, social activist and leader of the Arts and Crafts movement was extremely influential.

While he only lived at Kelmscott for a short period and it was never his primary residence, the house embodied everything he believed in, and he described it as 'heaven on Earth ... and such a garden!' Nature and gardens inspired many of his most famous designs. The garden has since been sympathetically reinterpreted to something that Morris, who was born on this day in 1834, would have recognized.

His famous dictum to 'Have nothing in your houses that you do not know to be useful, or believe to be beautiful', applies equally to a garden.

ST. DUNSTAN IN THE EAST CHURCH GARDEN, CITY OF LONDON, ENGLAND
Peaceful Sanctuary

Plants enhance the atmospheric ruins of St. Dunstan in the East. It's a quiet, reflective space in middle of the City.

This unique space is described by some Londoners as the most romantic garden in the city. Its ruined walls are great survivors. The first church on this site was built around 1100 and was badly damaged in the Great Fire of London of 1666. Only the tower and steeple of the Christopher Wren-designed replacement survived the Blitz of 1941.

After the war, a decision was made not to rebuild, as many old churches remain within the area. In 1967, the City of London Corporation decided to turn the ruins into this public garden. Seats, a fountain and historic walls draped with climbing plants enhance its hallowed atmosphere.

CHÂTEAU DE VILLANDRY, TOURS, FRANCE
Potager and Ornaments

Crisp symmetry of design is matched by the perfection of the produce. Villandry's famous *potager* is an extraordinary kitchen garden.

It's hard to believe that this immaculate formal French ornamental kitchen garden – a *potager* – was not created at the same time as the 16th-century château. When Spanish doctor and medical researcher Joachim Carvallo acquired the property in the early 1900s, the garden was in the English landscape style.

Carvallo created a series of formal terraces, with the garden's centrepiece – the beautiful and productive *potager* – at the lowest level. But equally meticulous are the Love Garden, Garden of the Crosses and the flower-filled Ornamental Garden. It resembles a huge, colourful and textured patchwork quilt.

LITTLE SPARTA, DUNSYRE, SOUTH LANARKSHIRE, SCOTLAND
An Artist's Garden

'The Present Order is the Disorder of the Future.' At Little Sparta, granite slabs carved with this quote attributed to French revolutionary Antoine de Saint Juste delineate the garden from the landscape of the Pentland Hills beyond.

In 1978, Ian Hamilton Finlay changed the name of his home and garden from Stonypath to Little Sparta. It reflected a shift from the garden as a place of recreation to a many layered work of art, full of sculptural objects with classical allusions and deeper meanings.

The garden appears united with the landscape. It is an artist's garden rather than a horticulturalist's. Finlay, who died on this day in 2006, believed that weeds such as rosebay willowherb (*Chamaenerion angustifolium*) had a place in the garden, but that the prolific self-seeder needed to be managed to prevent it going beyond the space allocated to it.

MONK'S HOUSE, EAST SUSSEX, ENGLAND
A Garden Writing Room of One's Own

Virginia and
Leonard's final
resting places are
in this garden.
Their lives are
marked by
two lime trees,
replacements for
the original pair
of elms, and with
plaques and busts.

Virginia Woolf walked through the garden to her writing lodge, a place she and her husband Leonard had built specially, and she used it for her work after it was completed at the end of 1936. She wrote in pen and ink, either standing up or sitting in a battered armchair, and looked out on the garden, noting what was in flower. She and Leonard had different approaches to gardening – he took the lead on design, choice of plants and growing them, while she found a way of turning weeding into a series of games.

Virginia wrote parts of her major novels such as *Mrs Dalloway* here and her final letter to her husband before she left to drown herself in the River Ouse on 28th March 1941.

BARTRAM'S GARDEN, PHILADELPHIA, USA
The Father of American Botany

This peaceful garden was once a hub of botanical activity, with newly discovered plants and seeds both arriving and being dispatched to botanists and collectors around the world.

John Bartram was an early botanist, horticulturalist and explorer of the North American colonies. Carl Linnaeus thought he was an exceptional botanist and he is regarded as the father of American botany. The garden he created was one of the first to plant a large collection of North American native plants. Bartram had contact with botanists around the world, and exotic species were sent to him and also planted in the garden. He established a nursery that supplied plants to George Washington and Thomas Jefferson for their gardens at Mount Vernon and Monticello respectively. Bartram introduced several hundred species into cultivation, with many sent to English botanists and plant collectors. He became a plant hunter and went to Florida, not part of the colonies at that time, and George III appointed him King's Botanist for North America in 1765, which paid him £50 a year.

THE COURTYARD OF THE HOSPITAL AT ARLES (1889), VINCENT VAN GOGH
A Garden in Yellow and Blue

Van Gogh's colour palette suggests the promise of spring, with new growth in the garden and more to come.

Vincent van Gogh's work shows the link between colour, mood and mental health. The artist was a patient at Arles hospital on several occasions in 1889. During periods of lucidity, he was allowed to paint outside his room, and this is one of several hospital paintings he made.

Although the tree branches are bare, colourful flowers, orange fish in the central circular pool and the bright columns convey an upbeat note, with people looking down into the garden. Born on this day in 1853, Van Gogh liked to paint everyday subjects; for him the act of painting was an emotional release.

GARDEN IN SCHOTEN, ANTWERP, BELGIUM
Cloud Hedge Garden

Wirtz walks
down a row of
his cloud-pruned
box hedges in this
photograph by
Dirk Heyman.

This was influential Belgian landscape architect and plantsman Jacques Wirtz's own garden. Parts of it are a nursery for the design studio, Wirtz International, which he ran with his sons Peter and Martin.

The box hedge was neglected when Wirtz took over the garden. Cloud pruning techniques turned it into the giant, roly-poly caterpillars that have become its most famous feature. Using classical techniques in innovative ways was a signature of Wirtz's work. The plant nursery at the garden includes some very large evergreen specimens used in design commissions.

COTTINGLEY FAIRIES, BRADFORD, WEST YORKSHIRE, ENGLAND
A Fairy Garden

The ingenuity and creativity of two girls fooled many for years, even acknowledged 'experts'.

In July 1917, 16-year-old Elsie Wright and her younger cousin Frances Griffiths photographed a fairy at Cottingley Beck, just beyond their garden. Wright used her father's camera and when he developed the image, he dismissed the fairy as a trick. He did the same with a second photo of her with a tiny gnome a few weeks later. But Elsie's mother who was inclined towards a greater belief in the supernatural, took the photographs to a spiritualism lecture and the fairy photos gradually became more widely known. The photos caused a sensation when published in magazines. Examination of their authenticity by various experts proved inconclusive. Arthur Conan Doyle – creator of the great deductive detective Sherlock Holmes – was a believer in spiritualism and wrote a story about the girls in the December 1920 issue of *Strand* magazine. The fairies' authenticity debate continued to the 1960s and was only fully debunked in the 1980s.

THE WAGNER GARDEN CARPET, BURRELL COLLECTION (17TH CENTURY)
Eternal Springtime Garden

This vision of eternal springtime could be rolled up to accompany its original owners on their travels. Unfurled, they were able to sit surrounded by a garden paradise.

Imagine a garden in a state of eternal springtime. This rare Persian carpet is the third oldest known, dating from the 17th century. It has been attributed through its weaving technique to Kirman in south-east Iran.

Two water channels running top to bottom linked by a central channel adjust the classic *chahar bagh* – four gardens that create a whole – design. A garden pavilion may have filled the central repaired area. Animals, birds, fish and insects mingle among flowers and leafy trees. It was a garden to be sat on when it was made.

BARNHILL, ISLE OF JURA, SCOTLAND
A Place of Perfect Isolation

The boundary line of the garden at Barnhill blends almost completely with the landscape of the Inner Hebrides.

'It was a bright cold day in April, and the clocks were striking thirteen.'

1984, GEORGE ORWELL

George Orwell wrote his classic novel *1984* looking out at this garden. He chose to rent Barnhill on the island of Jura for its location, ideal for writing without distractions. He described it as being 'in an extremely un-get-atable place'.

1984 was published in June 1949, less than a year before his death. Orwell's original title for the book was *The Last Man in Europe*. The garden at Barnhill is simply delineated by walls and fences, so remains part of the starkly beautiful landscape beyond. It feels as similarly remote as the novel's rejected title.

LONGWOOD GARDENS, WILMINGTON, DELAWARE, USA
From Quaker Farm to Fame

Longwood's magnificent Conservatory is the heart of the garden. It showcases a series of seasonal planting displays throughout the year.

It is hard to believe that Longwood, one of America's most famous gardens, was originally a humble Quaker farm. Businessman Pierre S. du Pont, who died on this day in 1954, created a series of garden 'districts' over a 30-year period after acquiring the estate in 1906.

The Conservatory is the centrepiece of the expansive horticultural experience and includes multiple areas of immaculate displays, many of which change with the seasons. There is always something extraordinary to see at Longwood.

FRICK COLLECTION SEVENTIETH STREET GARDEN, NEW YORK CITY, USA
A City Oasis

Even small public gardens such as this one trigger powerful emotions. The goal is for the museum and garden restoration to be completed in late 2024.

British garden designer Russell Page designed this garden in 1977 when the Frick Collection Museum opened an extension. It is a tranquil space enclosed by the museum walls and railings on the street side. With no public access, the garden can be viewed from the sidewalk or from inside the building. But in a busy city, the green oasis is widely appreciated.

Restoration of the museum and garden are currently in progress. Preservation architects Beyer Blinder Belle and renowned public garden designer Lynden Miller form the team to ensure Page's original vision for this garden endures. Galen Lee, the Frick's horticulturist, is also consulting. A direct link to Page, Lee has been in post since the designer recommended him for the position when the garden was first made.

PORTMEIRION, GWYNEDD, WALES
Number Six's Garden

The architecture of Portmeirion Village that is interwoven with gardens, terraces, courtyards and steps provided a suitable location for the 1960s series *The Prisoner*. See page 69 for Williams-Ellis's own garden.

Architect Sir Clough Williams-Ellis created this Italianate village over a 50-year period and hoped he would inspire others. It consists of an eclectic mix of ice-cream-coloured buildings in different architectural styles set in a woodland of sub-tropical plants on the slopes above a small harbour in North Wales. The village is dotted with small courtyards, fountains, pools and planted terraces. The Hotel Portmeirion opened in 1926; the last building, The Tollgate, was finished in 1976 when Williams-Ellis was 93.

Portmeirion became internationally famous as the mysterious location for the 1960s cult British TV series *The Prisoner*, which was shown in the USA, Australia and France and had many high-profile fans. Fans of the series and its mysterious leading character Number Six gather in Portmeirion each year for a convention.

ARLINGTON ROW, BIBURY, GLOUCESTERSHIRE, ENGLAND
A Photogenic Garden Street

Aristotle's words 'The whole is greater than the sum of its parts' aptly sum up the front gardens of Arlington Row.

Arlington Row in Bibury is one of the most photographed streets in the UK. The sum of its tiny planted areas combines to create a linear front garden that anchors the row of cottages.

Originally a 14th-century wool store, the buildings were converted to workers' lodgings in the 17th century. Visitors are charmed by its looks. It is said that when he visited Bibury in the early 1920s, Henry Ford liked it so much he wanted to buy the entire row, ship it to America and rebuild it as part of a theme-park project he had in mind. An image of Arlington Row was used as a security device for UK passports issued between 2010 and 2015.

ASHTON WOLD, NORTHAMPTONSHIRE, ENGLAND
Wildflower Meadow Garden

The meadows at Ashton Wold look natural, but were created by Rothschild with great care and skill over many years.

Ashton Wold is an exceptional example of wildflower and grassland gardening and reflects Miriam Rothschild's passion for the garden. A natural historian, zoologist, entomologist and parasitologist, she was a world authority on fleas and butterflies, and renowned for being a pioneer of nature conservation. When Rothschild inherited her family home, she turned the lawns into meadows using seeds collected from deserted airfields that had reverted to nature. Plants against the house grow as they would naturally. She famously helped create the wildflower meadow at King Charles's country seat Highgrove (see page 133), using a seed mix she developed called 'Farmer's Nightmare'.

FALLINGWATER, MILL RUN, PENNSYLVANIA, USA
A Home in Nature's Garden

A bold masterpiece, Fallingwater demonstrates Frank Lloyd Wright's theories on 'organic architecture'. The house is completely integrated with nature.

Fallingwater is one of the most famous modern houses in the world. It is also one of architect Frank Lloyd Wright's most renowned completed buildings that he designed during his long career, before his death on this day in 1959.

Built in 1935 for the Kaufmann family, the house appears to be part of the natural landscape around it, a waterfall of Bear Run stream seems to issue from beneath one of its large terraces. These projecting spaces are garden areas, places to sit surrounded by nature. They are supported by a complex cantilevering system – invisible but essential to the structure's survival.

OLD WESTBURY GARDENS, LONG ISLAND, NEW YORK, USA
The Great Gatsby Garden

Timeless Old Westbury Gardens have survived while many of its contemporary estates on Long Island have not.

Published on this day in 1925, the central character of *The Great Gatsby*, Jay Gatsby, has a mansion and garden described as 'blue'. Author F. Scott Fitzgerald uses colours to symbolize moods and emotions. Gatsby's garden is also the setting for significant events. Expanses of lawn are a metaphor for extreme wealth; seasons and plant life cycles track the underlying themes of decadence and doomed outcomes.

Old Westbury Gardens is one of the few surviving grand estates on Long Island. It exudes the status of the owners who created it in the early 20th century, similar to descriptions of Gatsby's lifestyle. It is easy to imagine well-dressed and bejewelled guests enjoying lavish entertainment on its terraces and lawns.

ARUNDEL CASTLE, ARUNDEL, WEST SUSSEX, ENGLAND
Tulip Festival

Tulips add to the procession of spring colour to the labyrinth at Arundel Castle.

April is Tulip Festival time at Arundel Castle Gardens, with fantastic displays throughout the many different areas. Colour schemes for each section are carefully planned the previous autumn and many thousands of tulips and other spring bulbs are planted.

A few months later, the labyrinth becomes a swirl of tulips and narcissus that invite a contemplative meander through the colourful flowers.

TUINEN MIEN RUYS, DEDEMSVAART, THE NETHERLANDS
A Demonstration Garden

These demonstration gardens show gardeners how to design and plant their plots in a forward-looking way that suits modern-day living.

Mien Ruys was one of the most influential landscape architects and garden designers of the 20th century. Born on this day in 1904, in the mid-1920s, she started to create small demonstration gardens at her father's nursery in the Netherlands.

After Ruys qualified she worked on a number of projects and published books and magazines. She continued to add to the gardens in Dedemsvaart, including the Water Garden in 1954. It looks surprisingly modern today. Ruys's gardens still inspire aspiring owners on how to design and plant their gardens and show the range of materials to make them both functional and beautiful.

SILENT SPRING (1962), RACHEL CARSON
An Influential Early Warning

Carson warned of a spring without birdsong if mankind continued to misuse pesticides. A world without nature and gardens is devoid of creative inspiration.

Rachel Carson worked as a marine biologist with the US Fish and Wildlife Service and wrote three books about the sea, including *The Sea Around Us* (1950). A passionate ecologist and conservationist, she predicted global warming. *Silent Spring* is one of the most influential books of the environmental movement. It was controversial because Carson spoke vehemently against the 'reckless and irresponsible poisoning of the world that man shares with other creatures ...'

Carson details how the link between the use of fungicides, herbicides and pesticides in the landscape has decimated wildlife in the USA, how it destroys relationships between plants, animals and the environment, and the tragic effects on human health and life. A collection of years of personal experience and findings from government agencies across the world underlines her message. *Silent Spring* warns of a world where there will be no dawn chorus, no insects to pollinate plants.

KEUKENHOF, LISSE, THE NETHERLANDS
The Ultimate Spring Bulb Garden

A stream of grape hyacinths flows through banks of bright daffodils and vibrant tulips. Spring bulbs make the boldest of statements at Keukenhof.

Keukenhof translates as 'kitchen garden', which reflects its 15th-century origins when Jacqueline of Bavaria gathered vegetables and herbs in the garden around her castle. The English landscape-style parkland seen at Keukenhof today is the result of an 1857 redesign by landscape architect Jan David Zocher.

Keukenhof is world-famous for its colourful displays of spring-flowering bulbs. Each autumn, 7 million bulbs are hand-planted over the three months before Christmas. The garden is only open for the short period of peak flowering.

THE *TITANIC* MEMORIAL GARDEN, BELFAST, NORTHERN IRELAND
A Garden of Ice and Water

The list of all those who lost their lives makes a powerful statement, particularly on this day, the anniversary of the loss of the *Titanic*.

Located on the east side of Belfast City Hall, this garden is a memorial to all those who perished when the RMS *Titanic* sank in the early hours of 15th April 1912. It opened on the 100th anniversary of the disaster. During the design stage of the plaque, it was discovered that other *Titanic* memorial sites did not show all the names of those lost. 'The Belfast List' of 1,512 people is definitive and includes passengers of all class of tickets, crew, musicians and postal workers. Planting was chosen to give particularly good springtime interest around the time of the disaster. Its restful colour theme reflects the shades of ice and water. Certain plants have a symbolic meaning: rosemary for remembrance, blue forget-me-nots and birch for rebirth or renewal.

The earlier Carrera marble monument was unveiled in 1920.

Left: Plant-covered pergolas make a green tunnel for the Parisian walkway.

Opposite top: Peto incorporated ancient stone features including pillars into his garden, Iford Manor.

Opposite bottom: Surprisingly, night skies near Dublin are dark enough for Grennan's spectacular discoveries.

COULÉE VERTE RENÉ-DUMONT, PARIS, FRANCE
A Parisian Strolling Garden

Inaugurated in 1993, Coulée verte René-Dumont was the world's first elevated garden walkway. Architect Philippe Mathieux and landscape architect Jacques Vergely created this linear garden on a converted section of mid-19th century disused viaduct on the Vincennes railway line. Today it is a 4.8-km (3-mi) stroll between the Bastille and Bois de Vincennes through trees, plants and reflecting pools. There are beautiful views across rooftops, with some sections being 10m (33ft) above street level. The walkway passes through a narrow gap between buildings, adding a sense of mystery and adventure.

IFORD MANOR, BRADFORD-ON-AVON, ENGLAND
A Garden with Ancient Stone

Harold Peto's design for his own garden at Iford Manor combines Italianate terraced areas, architectural stone elements and sculptures. Placement of retaining walls and features such as the Casita ('Little House') with columns dating from 1200, are in scale with the site and its topography. Peto thought that gardens needed stones as well as plants in balanced proportions.

DAVE GRENNAN'S GARDEN SHED/ OBSERVATORY, RAHENY, DUBLIN, IRELAND
A Stargazer's Garden

Amateur astronomer Dave Grennan discovered a spectacular supernova with his self-built telescope in his customized garden shed on this day in 2014. The shed's sliding roof is specifically designed to give his telescope optimum stargazing opportunities. His garden observatory continues the tradition of earlier astronomers (see page 81).

Darwin kept a count of the number of times he walked up and down the Sandwalk.

DOWN HOUSE, KENT, ENGLAND
Down the Garden Path

Charles Darwin had a passion for botany and understood that natural selection applied to plants as well as animals. He was not a gardener, employing others to care for the garden at Down House. Indeed, weeds and native plants were of more interest to him in developing his theories.

For Darwin, his garden was a place to think, observe, and conduct experiments. He created a Sandwalk along one of the boundaries with native trees including alder, birch, hazel, hornbeam and privet planted on one side and a long run of hollies along the other, more exposed side. Darwin, who died on this day in 1882, paced circuits of the Sandwalk as he formulated and evaluated his scientific theories. His family noticed he kept a count of each lap by kicking into the path one of a small pile of flint stones kept beside it.

It was a garden path where the journey was as significant as the destination.

QUEEN MARY'S DOLLS' HOUSE, WINDSOR CASTLE, ENGLAND
A Miniature Garden

Plants, seats and tools are all in scale. Everything in this garden remains in a state of peak perfection.

This miniature masterpiece was not designed to be played with. It was created to be a special feature of the Empire Exhibition of 1924 and as a gift to Queen Mary, inspired by her childhood friend and cousin of her husband King George V, Princess Marie Louise.

Another friend of the Princess, Edwin Lutyens, was the architect. The collaborative project involved hundreds of eminent designers, artists and craftspeople. Everything is at 1:12 scale. Gertrude Jekyll designed the garden. One area pulls out in a draw from the plinth of the house. Miniature plants are ever perfect and always in bloom. In 1925, the dolls' house went on display at Windsor Castle in a room specially designed by Lutyens.

Y BWTHYN BACH ('THE LITTLE COTTAGE'), ROYAL LODGE, WINDSOR, ENGLAND
The Little Cottage Garden

Princess Elizabeth enjoyed this cottage and its pretty garden. It remains a favourite with the youngest generation of her family.

This charming miniature cottage was a gift from the Welsh nation to Princess Elizabeth on her sixth birthday in 1932. Installed in the grounds of the Royal Lodge, Windsor, the simple garden reflects the time it was created. Understandably, it became a favourite place to play. Recently refurbished, it is still enjoyed by children of the royal family.

LIZ CHRISTY GARDEN, MANHATTAN, NEW YORK CITY, USA
The First Community Garden in New York City

Liz Christy relaxing in the garden in 1975.

This garden was a derelict site in 1973 when Liz Christy and a group of garden activists known as the Green Guerillas were throwing 'seed bombs' into vacant lots, and improving empty suitable spaces with plants. This unloved space became the first community garden in New York City, inspiring city gardeners to get involved and garden in the inner city. The community has fought attempts to sell off such spaces and it remains a gardened corner of a very busy city.

22nd April is celebrated as Earth Day. It marks the anniversary of the birth of the modern environmental movement.

ANNE HATHAWAY'S COTTAGE , STRATFORD-UPON-AVON, ENGLAND
A Tudor Garden

April bulbs in the garden of Anne Hathaway's Cottage, now a popular tourist destination.

Many scenes in Shakespeare's plays are set in gardens. The perfect backdrop to romantic scenes, he used them as places for leisurely strolls where conversations happen on a range of topics that work with the play's central theme, from serious political discussion to comedy.

Originally a farmhouse, this was Anne Hathaway's birthplace and remained in her family until the late 19th century when it was purchased by the Shakespeare Birthplace Trust. The garden is an evocation that suits the house rather than an historic representation of how it would have looked in Shakespeare's time. It's unlikely that the Bard ever lived here, but he may have visited Anne in her family home before they were married.

William Shakespeare is believed to have been born on the 23rd April. See also Twelfth Night (page 16), Much Ado About Nothing (page 38) and Macbeth (page 227).

COLLINGWOOD INGRAM GARDEN, THE GRANGE, BENENDEN, KENT, ENGLAND
The Great White Cherry Garden

Collingwood 'Cherry' Ingram named a form of *Prunus* 'Tai Haku' – Great White Cherry. He was instrumental in its reintroduction back into its native Japan. One of his original cuttings survives and can still be found in a Kyoto plant nursery.

Ornithologist and plant collector Collingwood Ingram developed the garden at The Grange from 1919 until his death in 1981. His interest in cherry trees began following a visit to Japan.

Cherry blossom – *sakura* – has been revered for centuries in Japan, but the popularity of a cloned cherry *Prunus × yedoensi* 'Somei-Yoshino' caused a serious decline in the number of different varieties available in the country. Ingram found endangered cherry varieties on later visits to Japan and took cuttings. His cultivation skills and new grafting techniques enabled him to grow cherries that were then reintroduced back into their native Japan. One of these was a form known as *akatsuki* (meaning 'dawn' or 'daybreak'), which had long since disappeared in Japan. Ingram recognized it as a form he had named 'Tai Haku', growing in another garden in Sussex. After initial failure, Ingram finally succeeded in sending viable cuttings back to Japan.

NYMANS, HAYWARDS HEATH, WEST SUSSEX, ENGLAND
A History Garden

Low hedging in this border echoes the design of the architectural detail above the old stone window in the ruined part of Nymans.

This garden is known for its collections of rare and unusual plants, fine views and the partially ruined house that was burnt out in 1947.

German-born businessman Ludwig Messel created the garden, and his son Lionel continued its development. Both were fine plantsmen. Spectacular white-flowered *Eucryphia × nymansensis* and the pale pink *Magnolia × loebneri* 'Leonard Messel' were both raised here.

This garden of horticultural highlights was donated to the National Trust in 1954.

BENTON END, HADLEIGH, SUFFOLK, ENGLAND
Cedric Morris's Garden

Several Inventions (oil on canvas, 1964) by Cedric Morris shows off a number of his own varieties of iris at his home in Benton End.

Sir Cedric Morris was an artist and plantsman. His home at Benton End became a centre of creativity, the home of the East Anglian School of Painting and Drawing, which he set up with his partner Arthur Lett Haines. This garden inspired his paintings and horticulture. A gifted horticulturalist, he grew plants not commonly seen in gardens and became widely known for breeding irises – many cultivars feature his name.

Morris's garden influenced many other gardeners and designers, including Beth Chatto. Benton End has recently been restored.

ROYAL BOTANIC GARDEN EDINBURGH, SCOTLAND
A Garden for Research

Brightly coloured blooms add splashes of spring colour to the rock garden.

Royal Botanic Garden Edinburgh is one of the finest botanic gardens, and its hillside location has magnificent views of the famous city skyline. Established in the 17th century on a small plot in the city centre, today it extends to around 28ha(70ac) of gardens 1.6km (1 mi) away in Inverleith. The rhododendron collection is a spring highlight of brightly coloured flowers that fill the air with fragrance, while the naturalistic rock garden spanned by a bridge has year-round interest. The tall Tropical Palm House has the garden's oldest palm planted at its centre.

This garden has an extensive living collection, herbarium, library and archive that support national and international research, education and conservation programmes. These make a vital contribution to broadening plant knowledge.

NEW YORK BOTANICAL GARDEN, BRONX, NEW YORK CITY, USA
Kew York

The Enid A. Haupt Conservatory was completed in 1902 and has been renovated several times.

New York Botanical Garden opened in on this day in 1891. It was inspired by a visit to Kew Gardens (see page 275) by eminent botanists Nathaniel Lord Britton and his wife Elizabeth a few years earlier. They believed a botanical garden was essential to advance the public understanding of plants and to lead in original plant-based research.

This is the largest garden in any city in the USA and is on a naturally picturesque site, with the Bronx River running through a rock gorge and 20ha (50ac) of old-growth forest. The garden's iconic conservatory has computer-controlled climate zones and makes a magnificent entrance.

MINACK THEATRE AND GARDENS, CORNWALL, ENGLAND
All the Garden's a Stage

The gardens are the perfect complement to Cade's extraordinary creation.

Rowena Cade bought the Minack headland in Cornwall in the 1920s and built her home on the clifftop. In 1929 she was involved with a theatre group that staged two Shakespeare plays in the open air and offered them her garden for their production of *The Tempest* the following year. Cade created a suitable stage and terraced seating on the steep cliff face, with helpers using mostly hand tools, even blasting rocky parts with dynamite. She worked alongside her gardener Billy Rawlings and the rest of the team; one misstep would have meant a 27-m (90-ft) fall into the sea.

These gardens were created after Cade's death and started with a small planted area around the café at the top of the theatre. This successful venture then developed into gardens that cover over 6,000 m₂ (1.5-ac) of space with a striking selection of subtropical plants that thrive among Minack's rocky outcrops and steep terraces.

YORK GATE, ADEL, NEAR LEEDS, WEST YORKSHIRE, ENGLAND
The Perfect Small Garden

Sybil Spencer was inspired by the late 19th-century Arts and Crafts movement in her planting.

York Gate was created between 1951 and 1994 by the Spencer family – Frederick and Sybil with their son Robin. They made the 0.4-ha (1-ac) garden feel much larger by dividing it into different rooms, each with a different atmosphere, linked by carefully planned vistas and circulation routes around the site. A real family garden, it is packed with creative ideas in both its hard landscaping and planting. On Sybil Spencer's death in 1994, the garden was donated to Perennial, a charity that supports people working in all areas of horticulture and their families. The legacy of the Spencer family lives on at this beautiful garden.

RHS GARDEN WISLEY, SURREY, ENGLAND
Society Garden

This classical canal was designed by Sir Geoffrey Jellicoe. Until recent years, the building housed RHS Wisley's laboratory.

Wisley is the home of the Royal Horticultural Society. Both house and garden were donated to the RHS in 1903 by Sir Thomas Hanbury and the society relocated from Chiswick in May 1904. But the garden was created earlier by George Fergusson Wilson, a former treasurer of the Society.

The garden has many different areas, including a large rock garden, impressive broadwalk through deep herbaceous borders, fruit fields and grounds where the Society holds trials every year of a variety of different types of plants, including flowering herbaceous, shrubs and vegetables.

Wisley continues to evolve, with considerable recent changes – a new entrance, new laboratory building and new garden areas.

ORANGE LILIES, BROADWAY (1911), ALFRED PARSONS
The Artist's Garden

Striking orange lilies stand out against paler shaded flowers and luxuriant foliage that are traditionally seen in Cotswold gardens.

Alfred Parsons was a notable garden artist during the late 19th and early 20th centuries, and he also wrote about them, submitting his work to gardening editors including William Robinson. Parsons was a well-known figure in the circle of artists based in Broadway village from the mid 1880s onwards. He was also a knowledgeable gardener and went on to make a garden around his new home in the village after this picture was painted. This oil painting shows a garden view that was typical of gardens of the period and area – full flower borders, trimmed topiary, a quiet summerhouse and a view to the countryside beyond.

A LA RONDE, EXMOUTH, DEVON, ENGLAND
A 360° Garden View

The unique house has 360° views all around.

The unique 16-sided house built in 1796 by two cousins, Jane and Mary Parminter, shapes this garden. A ten-year Grand Tour inspired them to build a home on their return with design elements they had seen, a place to display the many artefacts collected on their travels. In the late 18th century, it was not usual for unmarried women to build property.

Unusually shaped windows look out onto the garden, which is cottage style in places. A platform atop the central core of the house like a crow's nest gives fine views over the Exe estuary. Mary survived the longest; her detailed will preserved the house and contents intact and allowed only unmarried kinswomen to inherit.

ROOM OUTSIDE: A NEW APPROACH TO GARDEN DESIGN (1969), JOHN BROOKES
An Outdoor Living Room

John Brookes made his home in the renovated stables at Denmans and named it 'Clock House' (see page 287). He designed the garden with a terrace that was a 'room outside' his kitchen.

In his book *Room Outside*, the 'new' approach to garden design set out by John Brookes is to see the garden as an outdoor living room. One of the first to put people above plants in British gardens, Brookes regarded American landscape architect Thomas Church as his design guru and was inspired by his book *Gardens are for People* (see page 262).

Brookes advocated that providing more privacy and shelter would make gardens more useful and usable all year round, despite the British climate, and advised choosing plants that fulfilled a purpose first and foremost. Good garden design was an essential part of the solution. The way in which the British public have embraced gardens as outdoor living spaces is part of Brookes's enduring legacy.

PETTIFERS, BANBURY, OXFORDSHIRE, ENGLAND
A Garden for All Seasons

This photograph by Clive Nichols captures the harmony of the garden at Pettifers with its landscape beyond.

Gina Price has worked on this garden since 1984 and developed a passion for plants in the process. Untrained as a designer, her garden displays her considerable skills. Pettifers has a townhouse garden at the front and country house garden at the rear, with descending changes of levels that acknowledge fine views to the landscape beyond. Clipped hedges define garden spaces, with trimmed topiary shapes providing architectural structure. It is a garden for all seasons: a rich jewel colour palette of spring and summer flowers; strong evergreen plant masses give structural presence in winter, and are a backdrop to frosted stems of grasses and eryngiums. Pettifers is an inspirational and influential garden.

HIGHGROVE, TETBURY, GLOUCESTERSHIRE, ENGLAND
A Garden for a King

This 1994 photograph shows King Charles III (then Prince Charles) being interviewed in his garden. He was crowned in Westminster Abbey on 6th May 2023.

Highgrove's Thyme Walk is a major vista. Its avenue of golden yews is the only remaining legacy of the original garden when King Charles bought the property in 1980. They are now clipped in non-matching geometric shapes and backed by raised rectangles of pleached hornbeam – a hedge on stilts.

More than 20 different varieties of thyme were planted through the stony path, with later additions of marjoram and primroses. There is a timeless simplicity in these elements.

HIGHBURY SQUARE GARDENS, LONDON, ENGLAND
Pitch-Perfect Gardens

Abstract composition now holds attention in the space in which the movement of brightly clad football players did for many years.

Highbury Stadium in North London was home to the world-famous Arsenal Football Club for nearly 100 years until it closed on this day in 2006. When the club moved to a new stadium a short distance away in Holloway, the grounds were redeveloped into a new-style London square of contemporary gardens at the centre of apartments created in the listed stadium buildings.

These gardens were designed by Christopher Bradley-Hole, who was inspired by the historic architecture and pitch. The perimeter has been retained, and an abstract grid fills the central space with a series of structural hedges, screens and walls defining planted areas and water. Pitch-perfect gardens reflect the site's legacy.

LA FIESTA DE LOS PATIOS, CÓRDOBA, SPAIN
Patio Festival

The joy of brightly planted containers and gardening in small spaces is brilliantly evoked at this festival.

This annual festival and competition is celebrated over two weeks in May. The residents of the Andalusian city of Córdoba throw open the doors of their beautiful courtyards that are alive with fountains, pools, trees, and pots full of colourful flowers. The prize for the most beautiful patio is hotly contested. Many courtyards are communal growing areas amid living spaces; visitors are welcomed to the lively event into the night-time.

The festival began in 1918, but the idea of gardens in the central courtyard of a large house originates in ancient Greek and Roman architecture. Roman villas featured an enclosed courtyard garden, the *peristylium*, which was often colonnaded. The Moors also brought the courtyard *riad* to Spain – water was an essential element in both gardens. In hot cities like Córdoba, shaded patio courtyards help mitigate the summer heat, with temperatures cooler there than on the sizzling streets.

ERNEST WILSON MEMORIAL GARDEN, CHIPPING CAMPDEN, GLOUCESTERSHIRE, ENGLAND
A Plant Collector's Garden

A handerkerchief tree shades this peaceful walled garden in Chipping Campden.

This small, walled garden was created in 1976 to mark the centenary of the birth of Ernest Wilson, one of the greatest plant collectors of the early 20th century.

Born in Chipping Campden, Wilson introduced over 1,200 garden plants to the West during his career. His expeditions to China were so successful that he became known as 'Chinese' Wilson. An early notable introduction was the handkerchief tree (*Davidia involucrata*). Originally discovered by French missionary Père David in 1869, the first seeds collected failed to germinate. In 1904, Wilson tracked down a specimen from an earlier map, but the tree had been felled for timber. Fortunately, he found another one not far away, and was able to collect seeds that proved viable.

Wilson later became director of the Arnold Arboretum, Boston, USA; he died with his wife as the result of a car accident in 1930.

MEDWYN WILLIAMS'S GREENHOUSE, ANGLESEY, WALES
Grow Big (or Go Home)

Medwyn Williams measures an enormous onion at his business greenhouse.

Medwyn Williams is famed as an expert grower of giant vegetables, which have made him a Gold Medal-winner at the RHS Chelsea Flower Show on 13 occasions. His prize specimens are grown in greenhouses and polytunnels where soil, temperature and light levels can be managed. These measured, optimum conditions have been developed over a lifetime's experience of growing and showing vegetables in peak condition.

Williams is past chairman of the Royal Horticultural Society's Fruit, Vegetable and Herb Committee and president of the National Vegetable Society. His company supplies seeds for varieties that have proven records as prize winners at shows.

ROMAN DE LA ROSE (C.1230–1275)
The Romance of the Rose Garden

Red roses have long been associated with romantic love.

Written over a 50–year period in a series of illuminated manuscripts, *Le Roman de la Rose* – *The Romance of the Rose* – is an allegorical love poem of 21,000 lines on the 'whole art of love' that became very popular and influential first in France, then beyond. The lover is on a quest for the elusive Rose, which symbolizes his lady's love. His pursuit is written in dream form with illustrations that detail how gardens look, how they are used, particularly for leisure and romance, and the meaning of plants. In an age of chivalry, it was taken up as a manual for courtly love. Geoffrey Chaucer translated it into English a century later, titled *The Romaunt of the Rose*.

RHODODENDRON WOOD, LEITH HILL PLACE, SURREY, ENGLAND
Three Families, One Garden

The rhododendrons in full bloom. Leith Hill Place was donated to the National Trust by Ralph Vaughan Williams in 1944.

The childhood home of the renowned composer Ralph Vaughan Williams, the garden at Leith Hill Place links three famous families. Josiah Wedgwood III bought the house in 1847 after retiring from his famous pottery business. His wife Caroline, née Darwin, was the sister of Charles. The famous naturalist was a regular visitor and involved his nieces in earthworm experiments around the grounds – one of them was Margaret, the mother of Vaughan Williams. A 'wormstone' can be seen next to one of the path markers.

Caroline Wedgwood was a keen botanist and plantswoman. She planted many rhododendrons and azaleas beneath the trees along the driveway to the house to create a beautiful entrance. The mature tree canopy was severely damaged in the Great Storm in 1987. Clearance and restoration have returned it to an attractive woodland walk.

GRAVEL GARDEN, BETH CHATTO'S PLANTS & GARDENS, COLCHESTER, ESSEX, ENGLAND
A Sustainability Success Story

The Gravel Garden's ebb and flow of planting recall a drying watercourse and reflect the passing seasons.

It's hard to believe that prior to the winter of 1991, the Gravel Garden was once the car park for visitors to Beth Chatto's Plants & Gardens. Chatto originally created it as an experiment with drought-tolerant plants – Essex is one of the driest parts of the UK and this area is never watered.

Putting the right plant in the right place was central to Chatto's approach to gardening. She planted the area using only plants from her drought-tolerant lists. If plants died, they were replaced with others that proved better suited.

After planting, a layer of gravel was spread throughout – there are no defined edges. Colour and texture change with the seasons, with spent flowers and seedheads retained for winter effect and as wildlife food sources. An experiment in sustainability has become the garden's most inspirational area. Beth Chatto died on 13th May 2018, but her gardens thrive.

DR. JENNER'S TEMPLE OF VACCINIA, BERKELEY, GLOUCESTERSHIRE, ENGLAND
The Temple of Vaccinia

Jenner established a free vaccine clinic in this rustic garden hut, which is still known today as the Temple of Vaccinia.

On 14th May 1796 in this garden building, Dr. Edward Jenner administered what is now regarded as the first vaccination to James Phipps, the 8-year-old son of his gardener. Jenner's observations supported the belief held in rural communities that milkmaids who caught cowpox from the cows they milked were protected from deadlier smallpox.

Prior to this treatment, Jenner had taken samples from pustules on the hands of a milkmaid who had a rash caught from a cow suffering from cowpox. He then rubbed this material into scratches made on James Phipps's arms. Days later, the boy became mildly unwell with cowpox but fully recovered in a week. Jenner went on to prove this cowpox inoculation gave immunity to smallpox, but the medical community were initially reluctant to acknowledge his findings. Jenner named the process 'vaccination', from *vacca* – the Latin for cow.

No. 10 Downing Street Garden, London, England
The Prime Minister's Garden

The back garden of No. 10 Downing Street is rarely seen. It has been enjoyed by prime ministers and their families since the house became an official residence in 1735. Today, it occupies a 2,000-m₂ (.5-ac) 'L'-shaped space behind Nos. 10 and 11 and is enclosed by a brick wall. Its paved terrace, formal borders and garden benches around a lawn achieved notoriety in 2020 as the scene of alleged 'parties' during the Covid pandemic restrictions.

Azalea Garden, May 1956, Patrick Heron
Abstract Azaleas

Patrick Heron's abstract painting style conveys the effect of shimmering sunlight on swathes of azaleas in dazzling full bloom. One of a series of works produced in 1956 inspired by his Cornish garden, he painted a second series titled 'Garden Paintings' 30 years later.

Gardens in Cornwall have just the right acidic soil conditions for azaleas to produce a blaze of late spring colour.

Above: Planting at Gravetye still reflects William Robinson's approach.

Opposite top: If walls could talk this one would have very interesting tales to tell!

Opposite bottom: *Azalea Garden, May 1956*, (oil on canvas) Patrick Heron.

GRAVETYE MANOR, EAST GRINSTEAD, WEST SUSSEX, ENGLAND
A Wild Garden

William Robinson was an influential gardener and horticultural writer. Author of *The Wild Garden* (1870) and *The English Flower Garden* (1883), he was outspoken about his disapproval of garish Victorian carpet-bedding displays and refusal to use Latin plant names.

Robinson was a pioneering advocate for a naturalistic approach to gardening. As editor of garden magazines, he commissioned other leading gardeners such as Gertrude Jekyll to write for him. He gardened in line with his beliefs at his home, Gravetye Manor and the garden is maintained in the style he pioneered. Robinson died on this day in 1935.

LONGHOUSE RESERVE, EAST HAMPTON, LONG ISLAND, USA
The Red Garden

Larsen titled this work *Study in Heightened Perspective.*

This avenue of red painted cedar trunks interplanted with crimson azaleas is a modern piece of art by this garden's creator, Jack Lenor Larsen. A renowned textile designer, author and collector, Larsen built LongHouse in 1986 as an example in contemporary living with art and made his garden an equal art form. The site had previously been agricultural fields that were abandoned in the 19th century. Larsen designed the gardens as a series of gallery spaces for sculptures and artworks by other artists among lawns, pools of water near the house and woodland areas.

'GARDEN PARTY' (1980), HUNTLEY & PALMER BISCUIT TIN
An X-Rated Garden Party

This garden party scene became infamous when its background details were discovered, hence it is known as the rude, or X–rated biscuit tin!

British biscuit company Huntley & Palmer had a long tradition of producing limited-edition tins in a variety of novelty shapes. In 1980 a freelance artist was commissioned to produce this tin depicting a garden party in the style of well-known Victorian illustrator and artist Kate Greenaway.

Production went ahead without the company noticing that the artist had hidden some rude scenes among planted borders in the background. When these were noticed by retailers, the company hastily withdrew all remaining tins from sale and so it became highly collectable.

BARBARA HEPWORTH MUSEUM AND SCULPTURE GARDEN, ST. IVES, CORNWALL, ENGLAND
A Sculpture Garden

Hepworth positioned her work with respect to plant masses and buildings inside and beyond her garden.

Artist and sculptor Barbara Hepworth, who died tragically in a fire at her studio on this day in 1975, carefully considered the placement of her work in the garden outside her studio. She looked at plant masses and shapes within the garden as well as visible trees and buildings beyond it. Hepworth was aware how changes in light levels alter the perception of her sculptures and the space around them, and particularly how this is heightened outside by the direct light of the sun and moon.

The same principles apply to garden design and plant placement in all gardens, even those without a display of fine sculptures.

ROSMEAD GARDEN, NOTTING HILL, LONDON, ENGLAND
A Private Garden Square

Hugh Grant and
Julia Roberts
climbing over
Rosmead
Garden's railings
– not to be
copied by garden
visitors!

This garden was made famous by a scene in the film *Notting Hill*, released on this day in 1999, where starring couple Hugh Grant and Julia Roberts scale its railings at night to enjoy the atmosphere of the private communal space from inside.

Part of the Ladbroke Estate, Rosmead Garden was planned in 1823 as one of a series of crescent-shaped spaces within street layouts designed to create communal gardens to encourage community spirit – as with London's many garden squares. Non-residents can visit without climbing the fence as it is sometimes open for the annual Open Garden Squares Weekend.

LATIN GARDEN, RHS CHELSEA FLOWER SHOW, 1997
An Homage to Virgil

This modernist garden inspired by the life of Virgil reinterpreted classical gardens with exceptional results.

This groundbreaking show garden was designed by Christopher Bradley-Hole for London's annual RHS Chelsea Flower Show in 1997. Sleek and contemporary, it was based on classical principles and was inspired by the life of the poet Virgil. It evoked the three stages of the poet's life – childhood on a farm, fame in Rome and retirement to the country.

Bradley-Hole is known for his use of pure geometry in his work, including the golden rectangle, a design principal based on the golden ratio, an arrangement found in nature and used extensively in architecture, art and music. This garden marked a turning point in garden design at the famous flower show.

KIFTSGATE COURT, GLOUCESTERSHIRE, ENGLAND
A Garden for Generations

The simplicity of this green room, dark water and gently trickling fountain invite reflection.

This garden of steep banks with magnificent views has been developed by three generations of women. Until 1920 the garden was a small formal area around the house that Heather Muir decided to develop, aided and inspired by her friend and neighbour at nearby Hidcote, Lawrence Johnston (see pages 338–9). Her daughter Diany Binny continued, notably adding the semi-circular pool in the lower garden. Today, Anne Chambers continues this family gardening tradition. To celebrate the Millennium, she turned the tennis court into a simple water garden where Simon Allison's fountain of gilded metal leaves hovers above the black reflecting pool, allowing the water to trickle gently down. It is a calm garden space.

Kiftsgate is well known for old and rare rose species, particularly *Rosa filipes* 'Kiftsgate', which is given free rein to ramble up through mature trees.

TRENTHAM GARDENS, TRENTHAM, STOKE-ON-TRENT, ENGLAND
An Italian Garden

Expansive Trentham combines formal symmetry with contemporary planting in an 18th-century landscape setting.

This monumental garden is a reinterpretation of the Italian Flower Gardens at Trentham originally designed by Charles Barry in 1833. When the 2nd Duke of Sutherland sold Trentham Hall, a large part of it was demolished in 1911. The 18th-century landscaped grounds by Lancelot 'Capability' Brown became a public amenity space. A decision to restore the gardens was taken in the late 1990s.

This garden reopened on this day in 2004. Tom Stuart-Smith's design balances the formality of Barry's historic framework of parterres and pools with contemporary perennial planting based on ecological principles. It enhances the magnificent view to the lake. Rivers of Grass by Piet Oudolf and Nigel Dunnett-designed wildflower meadows are more recent additions to a garden that continues to evolve.

LEEDS CASTLE, NEAR MAIDSTONE, KENT, ENGLAND
A Home and Garden for Medieval Queens

The island setting and castle walls contribute to the special atmosphere of this garden.

This is one of the most romantic garden settings. The moated castle, built on two islands, has been home to a host of medieval queens, including Eleanor of Castile, Isabella and Margaret of France, Joan of Navarre and Catherine de Valois. Henry VIII owned the castle and transformed it for his first wife, Catherine of Aragon, while Elizabeth I was imprisoned here for a time before she finally acceded to the throne in 1558. The castle's last owner was an American heiress, Lady Olive Baillie, who bought it in 1926 and transformed it into a luxurious modern home – a beautiful country retreat with gardens to match.

WISTERIA, ENGLEFIELD (1954), STANLEY SPENCER
A Wisteria Landscape

Spencer captures the power of wisteria in full bloom to transform a garden. Here, the horse chestnut provides similar shaped but upright flowers.

Garden, landscape and flower paintings were the most popular of Stanley Spencer's paintings and were critically well-received. Spencer did not distinguish between the three categories and termed them all 'landscapes'. Known for the many paintings of his home village of Cookham in Berkshire, gardens featured in much of his work.

The combination of ceanothus, wisteria and horse chestnut in full late spring blossom dominates the architecture of this front garden.

WINFIELD HOUSE, REGENTS PARK, LONDON
The Garden of the US Ambassador

A cricket match between UK journalists and US journalists took place when former US Ambassador Matthew Barzun was in office. Lawns at Winfield House are more used to seeing US presidential helicopters landing.

Winfield House is the official residence of the United States Ambassador to the Court of St. James. Covering almost 5ha (12 ac), it is the second largest private garden in London after Buckingham Palace. American heiress Barbara Hutton bought a derelict Regency villa on this site in 1936. She named the house that replaced it after her grandfather, Frank Winfield Woolworth, founder of the retail empire.

Hutton moved out of the house during the Second World War and the house served various military uses. Damage was so considerable that on her return in 1946, she decided to gift the house to the US government, to be restored and used as the American ambassador's official residence. A token price of $1 made the 'purchase' official.

Restoration was completed in 1955, and by now the impressive interiors were matched by a beautiful garden with formal terraces and borders near the building moving to a more naturalistic style further away. Expansive lawns can accommodate the helicopters used by visiting US presidents who have stayed here and admired this 'secret' garden.

Memorial Day in the USA, where citizens remember those who have died while serving in the armed forces, is observed on the last Monday in May.

AUDLEY END, SAFFRON WALDON, ESSEX, ENGLAND
A Tea House on a Bridge

This bridge where tea can be taken was designed by Robert Adam in 1780. The Palladian-style structure spans the River Cam in an area designed specifically for entertaining, called the Elysian Garden. The view from the bridge looked out onto an informal flower garden – a new garden style at that time. Today, the Tea House Bridge survives, but many other garden buildings at Audley End have not.

PANGBOCHE, NEPAL
Greenhouse at Height

Pangboche lies in the spectacular scenery of the Khumbu Valley at 4,000 m (just over 13,000 ft) above sea level on the trail to the Base Camp for the ascent of Mount Everest. Usually, only potatoes can be grown at this altitude. But in recent years, villagers Ang Temba Sherpa and his wife Yangzee created a greenhouse in the grounds of their lodge that enables them to grow a surprisingly wide variety of salad crops and vegetables year-round.

Opposite top:
The 18th-century
Tea House Bridge
was designed
by neoclassical
architect and
designer Robert
Adam.

Opposite bottom:
The first successful
summit of Mount
Everest took place
on this day in 1953.

Right: The
laburnum walk at
Barnsley House
became one of
its most famous
features in the
1980s. Rosemary
Verey liked the
effect of fallen
yellow petals on
the paving below
and preferred not
to sweep them
away too speedily.

BARNSLEY HOUSE, CIRENCESTER, GLOUCESTERSHIRE, ENGLAND
An Arts and Crafts Garden

Garden designer Rosemary Verey and her husband David created this garden around their 17th-century home after they moved there in 1951. Rosemary developed a singular planting style, influenced by Arts and Crafts traditions. This garden became famous for its laburnum walk, knot garden and *potager* – a decorative kitchen garden with trained fruit trees and small beds of vegetables and herbs. It helped establish Verey's career and she became very influential. In the 1980s and 90s her clients included many famous garden owners in both the UK and USA. While Barnsley House is now a hotel and spa, the garden retains a strong sense of its creator.

BODNANT GARDEN, COLWYN BAY, WALES
Golden Tunnel Garden

B odnant means 'dwelling by a stream' in the Welsh language. This historic listed garden has been developed over 150 years by several generations of the same family with a passion for horticulture. One of its most famous features is the Laburnum Arch created in 1880.

The 55-m (188-ft) curving tunnel of *Laburnum × watereri* 'Vossii' becomes a spectacular feature in late spring and early summer, when its trailing golden flowers are in full bloom that usually last for around four weeks. Bodnant's visitor numbers double at this time of year.

The Laburnum Arch in flower

LEVENS HALL, KENDAL, CUMBRIA, ENGLAND
The Oldest Topiary Garden

Above: Rowe
painted Levens
Hall on several
occasions.

Opposite top:
Every plant in
this garden has
a medicinal link.

Opposite bottom:
Blanc first used
vertical walls of
planting in the
mid 1980s.

This painting of Levens Hall by Ernest Arthur Rowe was used as the frontispiece for the fifth edition of *The Art & Craft of Garden Making* by Thomas Mawson and E. Prentice Mawson. The influential book was first published by B. T. Batsford Ltd in 1900 and is regarded as the foundation of modern landscape architecture.

Rowe succeeded in making a living as an artist who specialized in painting gardens – not an easy career choice. He did not seek commissions but arranged visits to gardens of note, often through their head gardeners.

Rowe especially liked Levens Hall. It is acknowledged to be the world's oldest topiary garden, designed in 1694 by a former student of André Le Nôtre, Guillaume Beaumont, who was also James II's gardener. Levens Hall has had only ten head gardeners in charge of maintaining its topiary since it was created, a fact that may explain its survival in this original form.

THE ROYAL COLLEGE OF PHYSICIANS' GARDEN OF MEDICINAL PLANTS, LONDON, ENGLAND
A Medicinal Garden

This unique garden contains plants that link their medicinal uses from ancient Egyptian cultures to those used in today's prescription drugs. Over a thousand different species are grown, all with either a connection to medicinal use – in folk tradition, pharmaceutical drug or a plant fibre used to make dressings – or a Latin plant name linked to contributors to science or commemorating physicians.

OASIS D'ABOUKIR
A Vertical Garden

Patrick Blanc is a French botanist and inventor of the vertical garden – *mur végétal*. He has designed and planted green walls around the world for over 30 years.

Selecting plants that thrive in the same conditions is key to sustainability. Biodiverse urban vertical gardens on buildings help with climate adaptation and support wildlife.

HIGH LINE, NEW YORK CITY, USA
An Urban Garden

The High Line gives another perspective to the famous New York City skyline, particularly at night.

Today's High Line used to be known as the West Side Elevated Line when it was built in the early 1930s as a solution to the problem of transporting millions of tonnes of meat, dairy and other produce to city-centre food factories. Fifty years later, train use had dwindled, some stretches of the line were removed, and the remaining section was threatened with demolition, deemed to be an eyesore.

But nature intervened. Self-seeded wild plants turned the remaining structure into an urban green space. An organization, Friends of the High Line, was formed to campaign for it to be retained and repurposed as a green space accessible to the public. The design team was James Corner Field Operations, architects Diller Scofidio + Renfro with Piet Oudolf for planting design.

This 2.3-km (1.5-mi) linear urban greenspace has become very popular since it opened in stages between 2009 and this day in 2019.

SANDRINGHAM HOUSE GARDENS, NORFOLK, ENGLAND
A Royal Open Garden

Expansive lawn and planted terrace perfectly match the Victorian Sandringham House.

Since the Sandringham Estate was purchased by Edward VII and Queen Alexandra in 1863, each monarch has developed the gardens and grounds. George V agreed to participate in the first year of the National Garden Scheme by opening this garden to the public in 1927. His decision encouraged other owners of beautiful gardens around the country to follow his lead and open their garden gates to raise money for the Queen's Nursing Institute – district nurses.

It cost a shilling a head to visit this garden in 1927. Sandringham continues to open on certain days for the National Garden Scheme.

LE JARDIN PLUME, NORMANDY, FRANCE
The Feather Garden

This garden gives a new twist to the traditional orchard, with mown paths making a grid of meadows that reflect planted areas.

At Le Jardin Plume, Patrick and Sylvie Quibel have turned a field and old orchard into a beautiful contemporary garden in just under 30 years. It is named after the swathes of tall, feathery grasses that weave through abundant perennial planting, adding a sense of movement in the breeze.

A simple grid of repeating squares underpins the design. The D-Day landings took place on the beaches of Normandy on this day in 1944.

BLETCHLEY PARK, BLETCHLEY, BUCKINGHAMSHIRE, ENGLAND
Top-Secret Garden

It's hard to believe now that this garden played such an important role in wartime, and retained its secrets for many years.

In 1938, Bletchley Park House went from being a country home to a top-secret location for MI6's communications operations. The estate and garden became a network of numbered wooden buildings and brick ones designated by letters. Teams of mathematicians and codebreakers worked here to crack the Enigma code used by the Nazis for commercial, diplomatic and military communication. Alan Turing and his team built the Colossus computer that helped with the decryption of the Nazi's other main cipher system, the Lorenz cipher.

At its peak, 9,000 people worked at Bletchley Park, but their work only became famous years later. Turing, who died on this day in 1954, is most renowned for his work as a computer scientist; a test for artificial intelligence he later developed is still used today.

CHATSWORTH, BAKEWELL, DERBYSHIRE, ENGLAND
Gone But Not Forgotten

The experience gained at Chatsworth enabled Paxton to design the even larger glass structure for London's Great Exhibition of 1851 – a remarkable achievement as he was largely self-taught.

Joseph Paxton, who died on this day in 1865, was appointed as head gardener of Chatsworth in 1825. After a period of neglect, his innovative approach to design endures today throughout the gardens.

But it was Paxton's engineering skills that brought him great renown. He designed and built the Great Conservatory – sometimes known as the Great Stove – over four years, beginning in 1836. The innovative large iron and glass building was planted as a tropical garden. Creating suitable conditions for growing and propagating the giant water lily (*Victoria amazonica*) was a prime objective. Boilers to heat the glasshouse were fuelled by coal brought to site on a specially built small railway. Later, Paxton designed a larger structure for London's Great Exhibition of 1851.

Dismantled in 1920, as it was too expensive to run, the Great Conservatory remains a ghostly presence, the space defined by its thick stone wall base now planted as a maze.

GARDEN, NOTTING HILL GATE (1997), LUCIAN FREUD
Lucian Freud's Garden

Freud painted plant imperfections as they appear in nature. Spent flowers and curling leaves are part of the life cycle of all gardens.

British artist Lucian Freud (see also page 309) was famous for his portraits, but less well known for his many paintings of plants. He was not a gardener, but painted the view of his garden from his studio window. Freud painted what he saw; his plant paintings celebrate imperfections, such as yellow leaves and holes in foliage – things regarded as blemishes by others – and painted views of his garden in the same way. Some of his garden paintings focus on a buddleia's dying flowers and the general decay of herbaceous plants around it.

Rosa mulliganii makes a beautifully draped cover to the metal frame at the centre of the famous White Garden.

SISSINGHURST CASTLE GARDEN, NEAR CRANBROOK, KENT, ENGLAND
The White Garden

'For my own part, I am trying to make a grey, green, and white garden. This is an experiment which I ardently hope may be successful, though I doubt it. One's best ideas seldom play up in practice to one's expectations, especially in gardening ... Still, one hopes.'

VITA SACKVILLE-WEST

Sissinghurst is one of the most famous gardens in the world and has inspired countless gardeners. Its White Garden has been particularly influential. Vita (Victoria) Sackville-West and her husband Harold Nicholson were captivated by the collection of mainly Tudor buildings that were in an extremely dilapidated state when they bought the estate in 1930. Harold devised a master garden plan that created a series of outdoor rooms that linked the buildings and existing brick walls together, with hedges providing dividing structures. Vita expressed her passion for plants onto this blank canvas, with each area having a different style and plant colour palette. The garden was a consuming interest and developed throughout their lifetimes.

Vita wrote the 'In Your Garden' column for *The Observer* newspaper from 1946 to 1961. A novelist and poet rather than a professional gardener or horticulturist, she wrote from a personal perspective. Her conversational style encouraged and inspired readers, both novices and experienced gardeners alike. Gardeners take a leap of faith when planting their visions in late winter, a good time for major planting, as leaves and flowers are not fully revealed until summer. The White Garden today shows that Vita's hopes were handsomely fulfilled, and it is maintained in the spirit of her original vision.

HILL TOP, NEAR SAWREY, AMBLESIDE, CUMBRIA, ENGLAND
Beatrix Potter's Garden

This garden retains the spirit of the author, who was a keen gardener.

Author Beatrix Potter bought Hill Top with the royalties from her first book, *The Tale of Peter Rabbit*. Parts of the traditional cottage garden have an air of familiarity, as they inspired her delightful book illustrations. These have been useful in maintaining the garden as it was in her lifetime.

Potter was a gardener and an early conservationist. In addition to her much-loved books, her legacy was to leave the 1,600ha (4,000 ac) of land in the Lake District with 15 farms and the many cottages she acquired to the National Trust.

VILLA LANTE, BAGNAIA, ITALY
A Renaissance Garden

This fountain at Villa Lante feeds the water that keeps the dining table in front of it cool, a garden feature that was ahead of its time.

The garden at Villa Lante divides the house in two, showing how strictly the principles of garden design were followed here. Created for the 16th-century cardinal Gianfrancesco Gambara, it demonstrates the wealth and taste of the Italian Renaissance clergy.

Architect Giacomo Barozzi da Vignola designed this masterpiece. Many forms of water feature throughout the relatively small, terraced space. The famous water staircase has a cooling rill running down its centre. The cardinal's modern tastes included dining *al fresco*. A large stone dining table sits in shallow water, its central rill fed by the Fountain of the River Gods, enabling diners, food and drinks all to be kept cool.

GREAT DIXTER, NORTHIAM, RYE, EAST SUSSEX, ENGLAND
A Bold Garden

The meadow opposite the Long Border marks a move towards a looser, softer look in some areas.

Great Dixter is a forward-looking garden around a historic house. Christopher Lloyd's father Nathaniel created a series of enclosures defined by clipped yew hedges and topiary shapes. Against this Arts and Crafts backdrop, Christopher developed his bold approach to planting.

The 40-m (130-ft) Long Border is one of its most famous features. While it is deeper than many entire urban gardens, it provides inspiration for gardeners with plots of all sizes. Flowering shrubs add structure and form, while an eclectic mix of perennials, annuals and bulbs weave through, with contrasting foliage and flowers throughout the year.

In later years, Fergus Garrett worked as head gardener alongside Lloyd. They courted controversy when they replaced the traditional rose garden with exotic planting. Garrett and his team continue with Lloyd's approach since his death in 2006.

DAVID AUSTIN ROSE GARDEN, SHROPSHIRE, ENGLAND
An English Rose Garden

With five themed gardens, there are roses of all types here to suit all situations and colour preferences.

David Austin's interest in plants began in the late 1940s while in his teens and developed into a fascination with roses. Old roses were an initial passion and he progressed to breeding a new type of rose that added repeat flowering and a wider colour range – the benefits of modern roses.

The first rose he created was 'Constance Spry' ('Ausfirst'), released in 1961. After refining the breeding process, he named his new roses 'English Roses' in 1969. Another milestone was reached when he launched three 'English Roses' at the RHS Chelsea Flower Show in 1983.

These five themed gardens show the nursery's roses to perfection, with around 900 varieties ranging across climbing, shrub, species and old roses. The garden has received an Award of Excellence from the World Federation of Rose Societies.

NIGEL DUNNETT'S GARDEN, BRADFIELD, SHEFFIELD, ENGLAND
Meadow-Style Planting

Nigel Dunnett is Professor of Planting Design and Urban Horticulture in the Department of Landscape Architecture at Sheffield University. Of the many high-profile, mainly urban projects in his portfolio, the London Olympic Park gardens and landscape stand out. His own garden is an environment where he can experiment and observe the results of different planting methods. The sloping back garden has fine views and curving log stacks make sculptural walls.

FAIR LANE, DEARBORN, MICHIGAN, USA
A Garden for Parking

As founder of Ford Motor Company, Henry Ford revolutionized assembly-line car production, which expanded car ownership. Garden designs had to accommodate cars where practical – easier with custom-built new homes for the wealthy. Ford commissioned landscape designer Jens Jensen to add a sweeping driveway to his own garden, with shelter over the parking space beside the front door – a luxury for car owners.

LA ROSERAIE DU VAL-DE-MARNE, FRANCE
Roses upon Roses

Above: La Roseraie has 13 groups of roses, arranged roughly chronologically through the garden.

Opposite top: The curving logstacks of Nigel Dunnett's private garden

Opposite bottom: Henry Ford's driveway and parking canopy. The curbs are a modern addition.

This exceptional garden, also known as Roseraie de L'Haÿ, was the idea of wealthy businessman Jules Gravereaux. It was designed by Édouard Andre in the late 19th century. Today, more than 13,000 roses of many different species are grown, and the garden has an important collection of old roses.

Expansive pergolas laden with climbing roses span wide paths. Roses fill formal beds and are immaculately trained across traditional trelliswork. It's a heady place to be at peak bloom time in the middle of June.

CHÂTEAU DE MALMAISON, RUEIL-MALMAISON, FRANCE
Patroness of Roses

This watercolour depicts the goddess Flora adorning a bust of Joséphine with flowers. It was painted by Joséphine's *premier peintre* (first painter), Gérard, in 1806.

'My garden is the most beautiful thing in the world.'

EMPRESS JOSÉPHINE

Little remains of Joséphine's garden at Malmaison although it was justly famous and celebrated during her lifetime. Its naturalistic style contrasted starkly with the formality of nearby Versailles. She created a serpentine lake so that the landscaped garden could be seen on boat rides.

Joséphine collected many plants from around the world; some reflected the fact that she was born on Martinique. Her greenhouse was larger than those at the Jardins des Plantes, the national botanical garden in Paris.

But the name of Malmaison is indelibly linked to roses through her patronage of artist Pierre-Joseph Redouté. His masterpiece *Les Roses* comprised engravings of the 200 species grown in her garden.

THE BARN GARDEN, BEDMOND, HERTFORDSHIRE, ENGLAND
The Meadow Garden

This photograph by Andrea Jones shows button snakeroot, also known as rattlesnake master (*Eryngium yuccifolium*) with prairie blazing star (*Liatris pycnostachya*) in the Barn Garden's meadow.

Renowned landscape architect and garden designer Tom Stuart-Smith's own garden is modern with lush, naturalistic planting, reflecting his approach. The courtyard recalls his award-winning show gardens at the RHS Chelsea Flower Show, but it's a family garden, part experimentation and – as are most gardens – a work in progress.

Meadows hold a particular interest for Stuart-Smith. The native one, seeded 25 years ago, is low maintenance, cut once a year in late summer. The exotic or designed meadow is species-rich. James Hitchmough, Professor Emeritus at Sheffield University, advised on its planting – a repeat of a collaborative process on client projects. Its maintenance is more intensive than the native meadow, but lower than other planting. Since it was planted in 2011, Stuart-Smith has continued to add species as plant communities develop.

BUCKINGHAM PALACE GARDEN, LONDON, ENGLAND
The Royal Garden Party

The annual Royal Garden Party on the lawn at Buckingham Palace, 1926

Queen Victoria hosted the first Garden Party at Buckingham Palace in June 1868. Although initially described as 'breakfasts', they were held in the late afternoon and were a way for the queen to mingle socially after the death of Prince Albert.

The tradition endures; three Garden Parties are held at Buckingham Palace each summer, and one at the Palace of Holyroodhouse, Edinburgh. Around 30,000 guests are invited each year.

BIRR CASTLE DEMESNE, BIRR, COUNTY OFFALY, IRELAND
An Astronomer's Garden

Surrounding mature trees offset the scale of the historic giant telescope, Leviathan.

Science and engineering feats are on equal par with horticultural interest here in the garden of the 7th Earl of Rosse and his family. Leviathan, the great telescope built by the 3rd Earl, William Parsons, made this a centre of the world's astronomical community in the mid-19th century. This tradition continues with the cutting-edge astrophysics observing facility, Irish Low Frequency Array (I–LOFAR).

Around these scientific features, the formal gardens have the tallest box hedges in the world, and a fine collection of rare trees and shrubs. The current earl and countess continue the family tradition of plant hunting; recent expeditions include Bhutan, China, Kyrgyzstan and New Zealand.

DYLAN THOMAS'S WRITING SHED, LAUGHARNE, WALES
An Inspirational Coastal View

Thomas's writing shed has beautiful estuary views.

Dylan Thomas's writing shed was a former garage at the top of the steep slope above his home, The Boathouse, for the last four years of his short life. Although he had the stability of a permanent home due to a generous benefactor, wet coastal weather was not to his liking. The beautiful view of three estuaries with their changing tidal landscapes and the Gower coast beyond inspired his poem *Over Sir John's Hill* and finished his famous play for voices here – *Under Milk Wood*. Thomas's 'word splashed room' inspired other writers of his generation to create their own writing rooms away from the house, notably Roald Dahl (see page 259).

HONEY, I SHRUNK THE KIDS (1989)
An Ant's-Eye View

Simple tasks shown from a bug's-eye perspective can encourage changes to gardening methods and different ways of thinking.

An ordinary family garden becomes a treacherous jungle when the simple act of retrieving their baseball from a neighbour's back yard results in a group of teenagers accidentally being miniaturized by an inventor's experimental machine in this film that was released in the US on this day in 1989. It was released on 9th February 1990 in the UK.

This highlights the perspective of garden ground-dwellers, such as ants and beetles. Casually done, ordinary tasks such as watering with a hose and the resulting puddles, can be life-threatening for some creatures who are part of a garden's ecosystem.

THE ROSE GARDEN, MOTTISFONT ABBEY, HAMPSHIRE, ENGLAND
A Garden for Midsummer

This bench would be the perfect place to sit and enjoy the roses on a warm June evening.

This famous rose garden is a part of the gardens at historic Mottisfont Abbey. The National Collection of pre-1900 old fashioned roses was established here in the walled garden in 1972 by renowned rose expert Graham Stuart Thomas. Peak flowering time is usually in the last two weeks of June, but is dependent on the weather during that year. Old-fashioned roses usually only flower once a year, unlike modern species. A perfect time to visit is on a midsummer evening when residual heat radiates from sun-baked walls and heightens the roses' fragrance.

KNEPP CASTLE WALLED GARDEN, HORSHAM, WEST SUSSEX, ENGLAND
The Rewilded Garden

Rewilding a garden involves a mind shift away from traditional gardening. Knepp's gardeners play an important part in managing the ongoing experiment.

This pioneering project at the Knepp Estate began in 2001. Attention turned to rewilding the walled garden adjoining the castle in 2019. To help bring the experiment in maximizing biodiversity into the garden, designer Tom Stuart-Smith devised a master plan supported by a team of expert collaborators: Professor James Hitchmough, Professor Mick Crawley, Jekka McVicar and Charlie Harpur.

Rewilding a garden requires habitat regeneration. The previously flat pool garden was 'roughed up' with small peaks and troughs to create a range of habitats that support different ecologies of plants and wildlife, and the planting scheme was designed to increase the species diversity of flowering plants. A mixture of crushed concrete and sharp sand covers the ground, with areas of richer soil given just a light dusting of sand, while 'dirty paths' encourage self-seeding, which can be edited if one species dominates.

FILOLI, WOODSIDE, CALIFORNIA, USA
The Dynasty Garden

A clipped yew hedge defines the Sunken Garden at Filoli. Colourful planting reflects the season.

Filoli had a starring role when it appeared as the exterior of the Carrington mansion in the 1980s TV series *Dynasty*. But it is located in the hills of northern California rather than Colorado, the home state of the original Carringtons.

Owner William Bowers Bourn commissioned designer Bruce Porter to retain a sense of seclusion and privacy in the garden. Trimmed hedges and brick walls define rooms, including Italianate terraces and a sunken garden, yet the garden retains views to the landscape beyond. Now owned by the National Trust for Historic Preservation, it is immaculately maintained, and not far from Silicon Valley to the south and the San Andreas Fault to the north.

SCONE PALACE GARDENS, PERTH, SCOTLAND
The Important Contribution of Plant Hunters

The Douglas fir in the grounds of Scone Palace. Being a plant hunter was dangerous – at one time, most plant hunters died within one year of starting the job.

Scone Palace was the Crowning Place of the Scottish Kings and the original home of the famous Stone of Scone. The gardens and grounds are similarly steeped in history. David Douglas (1799–1834) was born locally and started his career here as an apprentice. He went on to become an explorer and plant hunter. Douglas survived 10 years of long, physically punishing expeditions through North America, before he died at the age of just 35. His body was discovered in a Hawaiian pit that was dug to trap wild cattle. One had fallen in earlier and gored Douglas to death.

A pavilion and garden trail bearing Douglas's name mark his important link with this garden. A Douglas fir (*Pseudotsuga menziesii*) he introduced from North America still stands here. Other notable garden plant introductions he made include lupins, phlox, sunflowers, California poppy, poached egg flower, mimulus, flowering currant and snowberry.

GARDENS BY THE BAY, SINGAPORE
Supersized Gardens

Lighting adds yet more drama to the famous Supertrees.

Bay South is one of the three vast nature parks comprising Gardens by the Bay in Singapore's central region. Everything in this garden is supersized – from the world's largest glasshouse to the iconic metal Supertrees.

There's something in bloom every day of the year; out of sight, pioneering technology helps make the garden sustainable. In Singapore's climate, Cloud Forest Conservatory is cooled to suit the conditions required by the plants inside. Visitors get a bird's-eye view of the gardens from the Supertree Observatory. It's a unique garden.

THE GRASSLANDS GARDEN, HORNIMAN MUSEUM AND GARDENS, LONDON, ENGLAND
Museum Gardens

Planting in the Grasslands Garden has been chosen to link with the World Gallery exhibit inside the museum.

The Grasslands Garden is a living display of plants that link to the anthropology and natural history exhibits inside the museum. It is a naturalistic meadow that combines plants from South Africa and North America and was designed by Dr. James Hitchmough in consultation with the museum's Gardens team who grew the plants. Its informality contrasts with the older, more traditional garden areas around the museum, which opened on this day in 1901.

REBECCA (1938), DAPHNE DU MAURIER
Manderley

'*Last night I dreamt I went to Manderley again.*'

REBECCA, DAPHNE DU MAURIER

One of the most famous first lines in literature hooks the reader's interest immediately, making them want to discover what has turned a former 'jewel' into a lost garden, full of decay and overgrown plants.

Maxim de Winter's second wife is the unnamed narrator whose dream reveals a home and garden dominated by the memory of his dead first wife, Rebecca. Great bushes of bright red rhododendrons massed in the garden were her particular love. When stems of the richly coloured blooms are displayed in a single room in the house, it's as if they embody Rebecca's lingering ghostly, all-pervading presence. Daphne du Maurier was inspired by a real house, Menabilly, which she lived in after *Rebecca* was published.

BATEMAN'S, BURWASH, EAST SUSSEX, ENGLAND
The Glory of the Garden

This watercolour
shows the house
and garden as it
was in Kipling's
time. It was
painted by Sir
Edward John
Poynter in 1913.

Our England is a garden, and such gardens are not made
By singing:– 'Oh, how beautiful!' and sitting in the shade,
While better men than we go out and start their working lives
At grubbing weeds from gravel-paths with broken dinner-knives.

FROM 'THE GLORY OF THE GARDEN' (1911)

Rudyard Kipling lived at Bateman's from 1902 until his death in 1936. In 1907, he became the first English-language author to win the Nobel Prize in Literature. Kipling spent his prize money on his family and designed much of the garden at Bateman's, creating an Arts and Crafts setting that blends well with the 17th-century house. He created a garden for his children to play in, for family and friends to enjoy. Kipling's writing desk looked over another garden area. It inspired him to write the poem 'The Glory of The Garden'.

FLORE–ALPE BOTANICAL GARDEN, SWITZERLAND
A True Alpine Garden

The Valais Alps are the perfect backdrop to this garden of alpine plants. At 1,500m (4,920ft) above sea level, paths meander through rock gardens and across small bridges that span water features. The garden is planted with 4,000 species that include local flora together with specimens from the world's other mountainous regions. Research is ongoing into the relationship between high mountain ecosystems and the environment. A traditional timber chalet lies at the heart of the garden.

MUNSTEAD WOOD, GODALMING, SURREY, ENGLAND
Gertrude Jekyll's Garden

Above: Munstead Wood's herbaceous borders, painted by Helen Allingham in 1903.

Opposite: Alpine plants are perfectly matched to their rocky alpine garden setting.

'Show me your spaces and I will tell you what plants to get for them.'
GERTRUDE JEKYLL (1900)

Architect Edwin Lutyens designed the house at Munstead Wood so that most ground-floor rooms had access out into his client's garden. Gertrude Jekyll's partnership with Lutyens became one of the most influential in early 20th-century garden design.

A trained artist, Jekyll turned to gardening in middle age when her already poor eyesight deteriorated. In addition to her work with Lutyens, she wrote extensively on colour, planting gardens and gardening in a naturalistic style. To ensure four seasons of highlights, she advocated dividing gardens into areas and planting each space with plants that peaked around the same time.

MONTICELLO, CHARLOTTESVILLE, VIRGINIA, USA
Thomas Jefferson's Garden

This kitchen garden is not hidden behind tall walls. The terrace enjoys views of the surrounding landscape.

'I am constantly in my garden or farm, as exclusively employed out of doors as I was within doors when at Washington, and I find myself infinitely happier in my new mode of life.'

THOMAS JEFFERSON (1809)

Thomas Jefferson was principal author of the Declaration of Independence, a statesman and the 3rd president of the USA. As a gardener, he was influenced by the years he lived in France as American minister to the court of Louis XVI, and also his tours of English gardens.

This productive, attractive garden was designed to be viewed, rather than hidden behind high walls. The series of terraces continue down into a large orchard. After finishing his second term of office, Jefferson was very happy to retire to his garden and estate and died on this day in 1826. The 4th July is also celebrated as Independence Day in the USA.

THE WHITE HOUSE, WASHINGTON DC, USA
The Rose Garden

Countless press conferences and events hosting visiting heads of state have made this garden globally famous. The garden has been revitalized several times, as plants age, but still reflects the 1961 design principles.

President John F. Kennedy decided that the garden at the White House needed a revamp following a 1961 state visit to France, with fleeting stops in Austria and England. His garden was no match for those he had seen at other official residences during his trip.

The Rose Garden's location near the Oval Office made it ideal for reimagining as an attractive space to hold official events. The president chose family friend Rachel 'Bunny' Lambert Mellon to lead the project. A knowledgeable amateur gardener and horticulturalist, she developed a simple, classic plan with designer Perry Guillot that created an outdoor room. The garden enhanced the architecture, linking two colonnaded sides, the main building and the rest of the garden beyond.

Large steps double as a platform near the Oval Office. The lawn is large enough to hold 1,000 people, yet small enough to be covered by a marquee.

LOGAN BOTANIC GARDEN, PORT LOGAN, STRANRAER, SCOTLAND
Scotland's Exotic Garden

Scotland's most exotic garden in full flower.

Located on the south-western tip of Scotland, Logan Botanic Garden is a slightly remote secret garden. It is also surprising to find this most exotic of gardens in such a northerly location. The warming Gulf Stream provides ideal conditions for plants from Australia, New Zealand, South and Central America and Southern Africa to thrive outside, giving this garden a distinctive atmosphere. In a peaceful, natural setting, garden highlights include a eucalyptus grove, a huge stand of giant rhubarb-like Gunnera that towers over visitors' heads and a forest of palm trees and tree ferns.

Logan Botanic Garden has been a regional Garden of the Royal Botanic Garden Edinburgh since 1969.

THE MOUNT, LENOX, MASSACHUSETTS, USA
Edith Wharton's Garden

The footprint of the building balances with the formal garden boundaries, demonstrating the author's approach to design.

'I am amazed at the success of my efforts. Decidedly, I'm a better landscape gardener than novelist, and this place, every line of which is my own work, far surpasses The House of Mirth.*'*

EDITH WHARTON (1911)

The Mount was built for author Edith Wharton in 1902. Her design for its garden reflects her ideas of what a garden was and what it should look like.

For Wharton, gardens were architectural, just like houses. The series of outdoor rooms created should be in harmony with both house and surrounding landscape – as this garden shows.

Wharton was an influential 'tastemaker' in addition to being a successful writer. Her book *Italian Villas and Their Gardens* (1904) expanded her ideas. She made two other gardens for her homes in France (see page 229).

CLIVEDEN, TAPLOW, BERKSHIRE, ENGLAND
A Scandalous Garden

A scene of many parties in the past, now a more tranquil setting for a swim and lounging in the sun.

Cliveden is famous for the spectacular panoramic view from the Parterre. On this day in 1961, the former home of the Astor family achieved notoriety when 19-year-old Christine Keeler met John Profumo, Secretary of State for War, in the outdoor swimming pool. A chance meeting at a party sparked an affair that caused a huge scandal that rocked the UK government, as Keeler was also the mistress of a suspected Russian spy.

This garden has often been used as a location for films. In 1965, part of the Beatles film *Help!* was filmed here. In between scenes, the Fab Four held races with the film crew across the Parterre.

TENNIS AT HERTINGFORDBURY (1910), SPENCER FREDERICK GORE
Game, Set and Match

Tennis at Hertingfordbury (oil on canvas, 1910), Spencer Frederick Gore.

The invention of the mechanical lawn mower (see page 246) turned gardens into places for taking exercise. Games that could be played on lawns became very popular from around the 1870s onwards.

This game of tennis took place in the garden of the artist's mother in rural Hertfordshire. Spencer Frederick Gore painted this garden frequently; landscapes and interior music hall scenes were other popular subjects. Gore's sister was the lone player, and it is unusual that no partner or opponent is shown. Lawn tennis was a favourite family game. The artist's father, Spencer William Gore, won the Gentleman's Singles title at the first Lawn Tennis Championships held at the All England Lawn Tennis & Croquet Club – the tournament we now know as Wimbledon. The week-long tournament started on 9th July 1877, but the finals were not played until 19th July, as they were delayed by rain.

195

19TH CENTURY GARDEN
BIDDULPH GRANGE

BIDDULPH GRANGE, STAFFORDSHIRE, ENGLAND
A Worldly Garden

This UK postage stamp, issued in 1983, shows the pair of sphinxes that guard the entrance to the Egyptian Garden at Biddulph Grange.

This garden is a journey around the globe. Its creator, landowner and merchant James Bateman, was an enthusiastic horticulturalist with the wealth to make a garden where his extensive plant collections could be displayed in a series of linked spaces, each representing a different country or style of garden. Most notable are China, Egypt, Himalayan Glen and Cheshire Cottage Garden.

Bateman employed plant collectors who travelled the world on his behalf throughout his 20 years of garden making. After he moved out, his son took over, but sold the house in 1872. The garden decayed until a large restoration project over 100 years later, but this is a continuous process in a garden of this age and scale.

JARDINS DE MÉTIS, QUÉBEC, CANADA
A Blue Garden

The Blue Poppy Glade usually reaches peak flowering in the first two weeks of July.

This garden full of horticultural interest is remarkable for several reasons. It is one of the most northern gardens in North America, set in an isolated spruce forest location. It was created by Elsie Reford, who, in 1926, started on an extraordinary garden making project of at the age of 54, and remained undaunted by the many challenges she faced, not least her garden being hundreds of miles from plant nurseries and other sources of necessary supplies.

Reford grew around 3,000 different types of plants, including both native and exotic species, and chose plants that were best suited to her garden's unique conditions. The Himalayan blue poppy, *Meconopsis betonicifolia*, thrives here and the garden's famous Blue Poppy Glade is a swathe of azure blooms for approximately one month from the end of June.

GOLDING CONSTABLE'S FLOWER GARDEN (1815), JOHN CONSTABLE
Garden to Vase

Splashes of colour in the Constables' flower garden contrast with the surrounding rural village landscape.

Artist John Constable painted this garden from the upper floor of his family home in East Bergholt, Suffolk. Flower gardens were a new fashion of the early 19th century, and the artist's mother tended these ornamental borders. The clear boundaries of the garden contrast with the surrounding landscape, the subject matter for which Constable was most famous. This personal painting was never exhibited by the artist.

GOLDING CONSTABLE'S VEGETABLE GARDEN (1815), JOHN CONSTABLE
Garden to Table

In this shaded vegetable garden, the artist's strokes of paler shades highlights a productive growing space.

This painting by John Constable sets his family vegetable garden in the context of its village setting with the neighbours' plots and the landscape beyond. A gardener tended this large kitchen garden, which appears to have an abundance of produce. Painted from the upper floors of his parents' house, this was one of a series of more personal paintings that were never exhibited by the artist.

JARDIN DES TUILERIES, PARIS, FRANCE
Marie Antoinette's Refuge

Above: The
Tuileries has been
a popular public
garden for many
years.

Opposite top:
A curving rill of
water flowing
in and out of an
octagonal pool is
one of Rousham's
best-known
features.

Opposite bottom:
The King of Siam's
Garden in bloom.

This garden witnessed the historic revolutionary uprising of 1789, when Louis XVI and Marie Antoinette took refuge in the Tuileries Palace. It takes its name from the tile factories that occupied this location several hundred years earlier.

The garden was originally designed by the renowned André Le Nôtre; some of the layout, several pools and historic statues remain. The palace was destroyed during the Paris Commune, but its grounds remain, a popular large public garden, is also home to two cultural centres, the Jeu de Paume national gallery and the modern art gallery of the Musée de l'Orangerie, where eight of Monet's largest water lilies paintings are magnificently displayed.

ROUSHAM, BICESTER, OXFORDSHIRE, ENGLAND
A Georgian Masterpiece

Timeless Rousham is one of the most influential gardens in the UK, a favourite of top garden designers. It is one of the few 18th-century gardens to have avoided alteration, due to the fact that it remains in the ownership of the same family who built the house and commissioned William Kent to shape the landscape around it. Kent was one of the most celebrated landscape designers of the Georgian period and Rousham is widely considered to be his masterpiece.

16TH JULY

ETON COLLEGE GARDENS, BERKSHIRE, ENGLAND
A School Garden

Eton's fine gardens are not widely known. The school's collegiate buildings feature a series of spaces including the Provost's Garden, the Fellows' Garden and the King of Siam's Garden. This last garden was made in 1929 after a donation from old Etonian King Rama VII. The site of former stables, it has been renovated in the 2010s by designer James Alexander Sinclair.

CHELSEA PHYSIC GARDEN, LONDON, ENGLAND
The Apothecaries' Garden

Behind brick walls, this is something of a secret garden that retains a sense of history.

This garden was established in 1673 as the Apothecaries' Garden by the Worshipful Company of Apothecaries for growing plants that might have medicinal uses. It played an important part in learning how new plant discoveries grew, the conditions needed for successful cultivation and their usefulness. Being close to the River Thames made it a prime location for receiving plants brought back from around the world and it also benefits from a milder microclimate – the garden has the UK's largest fruiting olive tree. Notable head gardeners include Philip Miller, who served for nearly 50 years, during which time the number of garden plants grown in England almost doubled; William Forsyth, who created the pond rockery that still exists; and Robert Fortune, whose many changes also remain.

This important research garden with an illustrious history remains a special, slightly hidden oasis today.

A GAME OF CROQUET (1873), ÉDOUARD MANET
Garden Games

This game of croquet was not played on an immaculately mown lawn, the setting that is usually seen for it.

With the increase in garden ownership in the late 19th century, gardens became places for recreational pursuits as well as horticultural hobbies. The invention of the mechanical mower in 1830 also played an important part (see page 246). When Édouard Manet painted this impressionistic garden scene, croquet was a very fashionable game and women were allowed to play alongside men. But this was not an impromptu moment, the group was 'staged': the two men were a fellow artist and a friend, the women were two models who regularly posed for the Impressionists. It is a lived-in looking garden.

THE NEWT, CASTLE CARY, SOMERSET, ENGLAND
An Estate Garden

The Parabola lies at the heart of this garden, and has an apple tree maze.

The Newt gardens have had several iterations in the last 200 years. Formerly known as Hadspen House and home to the Hobhouse family, a Victorian ideal was revitalized by renowned garden designer Penelope Hobhouse in the 1970s. From the late 1980s, the Parabola walled garden was transformed into a living experiment of perennial planting for colour effects by Canadian plant experts Nori and Sandra Pope.

Since 2013, this garden has been transformed by French architect Patrice Taravella. The Parabola garden is productive and beautiful with its apple tree maze and central water feature. An interactive experience, The Story of Gardening, explores garden history, and famous gardens of the world can be visited in virtual reality pods. The estate's unusual name was inspired by a colony of great crested newts that live in the grounds.

LIFE ON MARS GARDEN (600 DAYS), RHS CHELSEA FLOWER SHOW, 2007
Green Red Planet

The Life on Mars garden won a gold medal and Best in Show at the RHS Chelsea Flower Show in 2007. We choose to feature it on the date of the first moon landing: 20th July 1969.

Is there life on Mars? While there remains no definitive answer, ongoing space exploration continues to expand our knowledge of the planets in the Solar System. Landscape architect Sarah Eberle spent eight years planning this show garden for the RHS Chelsea Flower Show in 2007. It was based on the idea of astronauts spending 600 days living on the planet – travel between Earth and Mars is only possible on a two-year cycle. The first manned landing on the Moon took place on this day in 1969.

Eberle took advice from space experts during her extensive research into the conditions on the Red Planet. The extraterrestrial look was balanced by each element being scientifically possible. Each plant chosen was either medicinal or edible, selected for scientific need rather than artistic effect, with water a precious resource that must be conserved.

Global warming resonates with gardeners' responsibilities on Earth.

CAUDRA SAN CRISTOBAL, MEXICO CITY, MEXICO
An Architectural Garden

The horse pool in front is a shallow basin, its white lining highlighting the transparency of the water. Unseen here, a large fountain constantly refreshes the pool and adds cooling sound effects to the courtyard.

'I don't divide architecture, landscape and gardening; to me, they are one.'

LUIS BARRAGÁN

Among the most influential architects of the 20th century, Luis Barragán described himself as a landscape architect who believed gardens were part of a house, and they should 'combine the poetic and the mysterious'. This is one of Barragán's most famous works. Part of a private estate, the huge rectangular courtyard includes a house, stables and ancillary buildings. Dividing space with stucco walls of different colours was one of Barragán's design signatures. This pink wall divides different parts of the estate. Its two portals or doorways are scaled to the height of horses with their riders.

Designed and built between 1966 and 1968, the surrounding area was quiet, semi-rural. While the relentless sprawl of Mexico City has altered the location, San Cristobal retains an aura of calm, as Barragán's original vision.

LOTUSLAND, MONTECITO, CALIFORNIA, USA
An Eclectic Garden

Giant clam shells form a cascade that spills into a pool edged with abalone shells in the Aloe Garden at Lotusland.

Polish-born opera singer Ganna Walska created this beautiful garden in just over 40 years. Much of her wealth came from her six marriages – money was no object in her garden making. She changed plans commissioned from designers to match her preferences and managed every aspect from design to planting – effectively she was head gardener.

Lotusland reflects Walska's passion and is one of the few survivors from Hollywood's golden era. It has 3,000 different plants from all over the world, giving different areas a distinctive atmosphere. When she died in 1984, she left her garden and wealth to the Ganna Walska Lotusland Foundation.

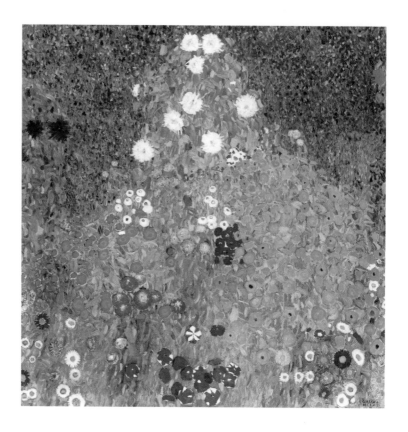

COTTAGE GARDEN (*BAUERNGARTEN*) (1905), GUSTAV KLIMT
Gustav's Garden

Cottage Garden (Bauerngarten) (oil on canvas, 1905), Gustav Klimt.

The Austrian Symbolist painter, Gustav Klimt, painted a series of garden paintings in his typical, impressionistic style that also expressed emotions. But different flower types are certainly distinguishable in this painting, including cottage garden favourites daisies, dahlias, petunias and the suggestion of a single deep blue delphinium.

JARDIN ETNOBOTANICO DE OAXACA, MEXICO
A Botanic Garden With a Difference

Mexican fence post cactus (*Pachycereus marginatus*) flanks a garden path. Its common name reflects the fact that it is traditionally planted to make a living fence.

Located near the historic landmark Santo Domingo church in Oaxaca, this site was part of the monastery grounds until it was occupied by the Mexican army for over 120 years. A government plan was devised to turn the space into a hotel and car park. But renowned artist Francisco Toledo led a local community group in lobbying for a garden that reflected the culture and people of the region.

Officially opened in 1998, the garden was designed by artists including Luis Zárate, Alejandro de Ávila and Toledo. It celebrates Oaxaca's native plant diversity and reflects the artistic and cultural traditions of the state and its place in the natural history of Mexico.

OXFORD BOTANIC GARDEN, ENGLAND
Lyra and Will's Garden

Ornamental planting combines with areas devoted to practical botany and research in this historic garden.

This is the UK's oldest botanic garden and one of the oldest scientific gardens in the world. Founded on this day in 1621, the walled area was originally a physic garden growing plants for medicinal research. The garden shows the importance of plants in the world. Changes that scientific research have brought to plant classification are reflected in the reconfiguration of formal taxonomic – family – beds.

But this garden successfully combines practical botany with aesthetic planting. Visitors are attracted to a bench in a corner of the Lower Garden, a significant location in Philip Pullman's *His Dark Materials* trilogy. When characters Lyra and Will realize they must separate forever, Lyra leads Will to this bench in his world that also exists in the same place in her world. This garden moves forwards, but acknowledges its important history.

SHAW'S CORNER, AYOT ST. LAWRENCE, HERTFORDSHIRE, ENGLAND
A Playwright's Garden

Shaw moved his specially adapted writing shed himself. A wall-mounted telephone indicates that he did not mind interruptions when at work.

Born on this day in 1856, Irish playwright George Bernard Shaw moved to Shaw's Corner when he was at the height of his fame. He walked to the bottom of the tranquil garden on the way to his famous rotating writing shed.

As Shaw liked to follow the sun as he worked, he had his writing shed mounted on a revolving mechanism so that it could be turned. He wrote many of his plays here.

NEWBY HALL, NORTH YORKSHIRE, ENGLAND
Bees and Bugs in the Country

Closely trimmed yew hedges form a dark backdrop to these exceptional herbaceous borders.

Since the 1920s, several generations of the Compton family have created the award-winning gardens at Newby Hall. This double herbaceous border is one of the garden's most famous features. At 172m (564ft), it is one of the longest in the country, and runs down a sloping north–south axis, from the house at the top to the River Ure at the bottom. In recent years, it has been revamped, as many plants were ready to be lifted, divided and replanted, and the colour scheme has been updated as part of this rejuvenation. Careful planning ensures there is colour from late spring to late summer, making it a haven for bees and butterflies.

Retained favourites including the milky bellflower (*Campanula lactiflora*) and delphiniums are interspersed with fresh introductions of architectural plants such as the cotton or Scottish thistle (*Onopordum acanthium*). Asters , dahlias and long-flowering *Geranium* 'Patricia' extend the display of richly coloured flowers through to the end of the season.

NOMURA INTERNATIONAL PLC, 1 ANGEL LANE, CITY OF LONDON, ENGLAND
Bees and Bugs in the City

Bean-supporting canes echo the shape of the Shard in this productive city garden.

This large rooftop garden combines biodiversity with a spectacular view of the City of London . Since 2011, the garden has been growing organic vegetables and a variety of flowering plants, which attract pollinators and birds. An area of green roof is home to beehives, which are maintained by the company's charity partners. Through hosted weekly visits in summer, employees have the opportunity to learn about the critical role of bees in the ecosystem, and also take part in the honey harvesting process, which takes place in July and August.

In recent years, a variety of invertebrate nesting habitats have been installed, including bee banks, log piles and nest boxes. These encourage solitary bees and a range of invertebrates to breed – another much-needed boost to urban biodiversity.

HAUSER + WIRTH GALLERY, BRUTON, SOMERSET, ENGLAND
Oudolf Field

A designed field of planting makes a statement in the surrounding countryside; its organic shapes shift with the seasons as they change.

This garden resembles a giant abstract tapestry that has been draped over the English landscape. Great swathes of perennial plants and ornamental grasses are the materials used by Dutch garden designer Piet Oudolf. Plant and leaf shape is as important as flower colour and size. The deterioration or senescence of spent flowers and seedheads continues textural effects into winter, and also provides a food source for birds and other wildlife.

Oudolf's contemporary approach develops the traditions of past master planting designers such as Gertrude Jekyll (see page 189) and Karl Foerster (see page 331). See page 288 for Oudolf's own garden.

A WOMAN AND CHILD IN A GARDEN (1883–4), BERTHE MORISOT
A Garden in Summer

A Woman and Child in a Garden (oil on canvas, 1883-4), Berthe Morisot.

Berthe Morisot's painting perfectly evokes the pleasure of spending a summer's afternoon in a garden. The focus is on the woman and child, while the garden is sketchily painted, suggesting summer haze or highlighting the importance of the subjects. Morisot's daughter plays with the sailing boat in the garden of the family's holiday house at Bougival in France.

Morisot trained at a time when women artists required a chaperone; her paintings reflect the life she lived, and private gardens were accessible, safe places to paint. She was married to Eugene Manet, brother of artist Édouard; and was one of the first women to paint men – her husband – in a domestic setting.

ROYAL CRESCENT, BATH, ENGLAND
The Dare-to-be-Different Street Garden

Royal Crescent is a popular location for filming, including Jane Austen's *Persuasion*, the 2008 film *The Duchess* starring Keira Knightley, and the Netflix series *Bridgerton*.

Royal Crescent in Bath is one of the most famous streets in the country and defines the city to people both in the UK and abroad. Designed by John Wood the Younger and built between 1767 and 1775, its 30 terraced houses are treated as one, with a ha-ha created to keep grazing animals out of garden areas across the front. Impeccable front gardens are mostly paved with large, planted containers.

In the 1970s, when the owner of No. 22 painted her front door primrose yellow instead of the traditional white it caused a controversy. Miss Amabel Wellesley-Colley defended herself through two enforcement notices and at a public inquiry, before it was decided her door could stay yellow. Subsequent owners have kept the colour, which distinguishes the house from its neighbours.

HOLYDAY (C.1876), JAMES TISSOT
Garden Tea party

Holyday (oil on canvas, c.1876), James Tissot

This tea party was painted by artist James Tissot in his garden in St. John's Wood, London, where he had moved after the fall of the Paris Commune in 1870. As befits the wealthy area, it is a grand garden with a formal, stone-edged pool enclosed by a tall colonnade and mature horse-chestnut tree. On this public holiday or holyday, the men are more casually dressed than the women. The sleeping older woman is suggestive of a chaperone failing in her duty to keep an eye on the younger members of the group, which at the time prompted some to consider the painting rather risqué or vulgar.

GORDON CASTLE WALLED GARDEN, FOCHABERS, MORAY, SCOTLAND
A Kitchen Garden

The view towards the Garden Cottage shows planting including white cosmos and sweetpeas.

Gordon Castle Walled Garden is one of the largest walled gardens in the UK, covering just over 3ha (8ac). From the late 1940s to the late 1980s, raspberries were commercially grown here, but the many fruit trees trained against the walls were pruned annually by a retired former gardener at the garden.

Current owners Angus and Zara Gordon Lennox have brought new life into this garden, based on a masterplan by garden designer Arne Maynard drawn up in 2011. His scheme combines links to the garden's past with forward-looking elements – original trained fruit trees and vegetables with meadows, cut flowers, a children's play area and a small amphitheatre for events.

GREAT MAYTHAM HALL, KENT, ENGLAND
An Inspirational Garden

Today, the garden that inspired *The Secret Garden* is a far cry from the neglected wilderness of the classic story.

'And the secret garden bloomed and bloomed and every morning revealed new miracles.'

THE SECRET GARDEN (1911), FRANCES HODGSON BURNETT

This walled garden inspired Frances Hodgson Burnett to write *The Secret Garden* (see opposite), but that was before it looked like this. Hodgson Burnett leased the house in 1898 and found a gate into an old, overgrown walled garden. When it was renovated around 1910 to a design by architect Edwin Lutyens with planting by Gertrude Jekyll, the original garden gate was bricked up. This garden has a romantic atmosphere, even though it is not the overgrown wilderness that inspired the famous book. Gardens reveal 'new miracles' every morning, as Hodgson Burnett wrote in *The Secret Garden*.

THE SECRET GARDEN (1911), FRANCES HODGSON BURNETT
An Inspired Garden

This illustration is from the first edition of *The Secret Garden*, published in August 1911.

For centuries and across different cultures, enclosed gardens have represented paradise on Earth. The idea that being shut off from the real world brings true freedom has universal appeal, as Mary finds in the story.

The Secret Garden is full of symbolism: orphan Mary is deemed to be a 'difficult' child. Born in India she is suddenly orphaned and sent to a country she does not know, to live with a widowed uncle she has never met, at his large Yorkshire estate. Left to her own devices, Mary discovers a secret walled garden by venturing through the overgrown outer thicket, but is frustrated from entering by a large, locked gate. A robin guides her to where the key to the garden is hidden. Finding the secret garden propels friendships with her delicate cousin Colin and Dickon, the gardener's boy.

The book symbolizes gardening as a form of redemption and the restorative powers of simply being in a cultivated, green space.

HORATIO'S GARDEN SOUTHWEST, SALISBURY DISTRICT HOSPITAL, WILTSHIRE, ENGLAND
A Healing Garden

Horatio's Gardens have wide paths and are surfaced with materials that make them accessible to all patients. Trees and shrubs give year round structure, while herbaceous plants reflect the changing of the seasons.

This garden is named after Horatio Chapple. At 17 years old, he planned to study medicine and volunteered at this spinal treatment centre in the school holidays. In 2011, his research among patients identified the need for a garden specifically designed to be fully accessible for all those with spinal injuries, who spend long periods of time in hospital. Tragically, he did not live to see this beautiful garden and the many benefits it brings. Horatio was killed that summer on this day while on an Arctic expedition. His camp in Svalbard was attacked by a polar bear and he lost his life while courageously fending off the bear so his friends might escape.

Cleve West designed this first Horatio's Garden. There are now seven others at spinal injury units across the UK, each designed by different garden designers and maintained by head gardeners with teams of volunteers.

Horatio Chapple died on 5th August 2011.

TRESCO ABBEY GARDEN, ISLES OF SCILLY, ENGLAND
A Subtropical English Garden

The Middle Terrace at Tresco Abbey Garden. The island enjoys a year-round mild climate.

It is hard to believe that Tresco Abbey Garden is just 48km (30mi) off the Cornish coast. In 1834, Augustus Smith built a home above the ruins of St. Nicholas Priory and started to create a garden for the house he called Tresco Abbey. This subtropical garden based around the priory ruins grows 20,000 plant species from 80 different countries on terraces Smith created on the sloping site. Striking exotic plants fill the space with colour, contrasting shapes and different textures, all revealed when walking the garden's winding cross paths and generous steps through its terraces. A survivor of icy temperatures that reduced planting to watery mush in 1987 and hurricane winds that decimated the original shelterbelt in 1990, this famous garden continues to delight and evolve.

BROUGHTON GRANGE, OXFORDSHIRE, ENGLAND
A Contemporary Walled Garden

This garden is one of the most photographed in the UK. It is often featured in magazines.

This garden was created in 2001 and contrasts with formal gardens of traditional borders, knot garden and rose parterres surrounding the house, which dates back to 1620. Tom Stuart-Smith was commissioned to design the 2.4-ha (6-acre) area that is walled on three sides. A series of three terraces of abundant perennial planting spreads colour down the slope towards the superb view of the surrounding countryside. A water tank, pools with stepping stones, canals and rills add reflected light and smooth texture. It is considered by many to be one of the best gardens to be made in the UK this century.

CHARLESTON, FIRLE, LEWES, EAST SUSSEX, ENGLAND
Bloomsbury in Sussex

Sculpture and bright planting fill the garden that was designed as a 'living painting'.

This garden in East Sussex was a muse to the artist Vanessa Bell and friend and fellow artist Duncan Grant. It was their country home, studio and gathering place for all their circle, the Bloomsbury Group. The living artwork garden was originally created in the 1920s. Bell and Grant lived at Charleston permanently later, and the garden has been restored after detailed research including hearing the childhood memories of those who grew up here including Angelica Garnett and Quentin Bell. Summer colours from garden flowers are echoed inside in the many hand-painted interior features.

THE GARDEN OF PEACE (JAPANESE GARDEN), UNESCO HEADQUARTERS, PARIS, FRANCE
A Garden Designed by an Artist

Above: The plants in this garden have been chosen to reflect Japan's natural landscape.

Opposite: Cawdor Castle's Flower Garden bathed in summer light.

American-Japanese sculptor Isamu Noguchi was commissioned to design this garden in 1956, when his skills were at their peak. Noguchi's design is a fusion of modernist principles with the traditional art of Japanese garden making. Donated by the government of Japan, it was the first garden to be created by an artist rather than garden specialist. In this tranquil space, the stone head known as the Nagasaki Angel, originally on the façade of the Urakami Church in Nagasaki, is displayed on a small, wall-mounted plinth. It miraculously survived the devastation of the atomic bomb dropped on the city on 9th August 1945.

CAWDOR CASTLE, NAIRN, SCOTLAND
The Thane of Cawdor's Garden

William Shakespeare wrote *The Tragedie of Macbeth* in 1606. The story on which it was based came from the history of the real Thane of Cawdor in the 11th century written by historian Raphael Holinshed. The 1587 edition of his book *The Chronicles of England, Scotelande, and Ireland,* was one of Shakespeare's favourite sources.

As the oldest parts of the castle date to the late 14th century, the play's King Duncan could not have been murdered here, nor could the witches have promised Macbeth the title Thane of Cawdor, and prophesied his accession to the Scottish throne.

Despite this reality, castle and garden have a very romantic atmosphere. Shakespeare may have chosen the story as a nod to the 'new' King James I – James VI of Scotland – who acceded to the English throne in 1603.

EAST LAMBROOK MANOR, SOMERSET, ENGLAND
A Cottage Garden

Above: A paved
path runs through
heavily planted
borders

Opposite top:
Edith Wharton in
her garden in 1929.

Opposite bottom:
This inspirational
planting style
shows that
planting can
be beautiful,
sustainable
and lower
maintenance.

Margery Fish made this cottage-style garden later in her life. Created during the 1950s, it references older times. Fish championed cottage-style perennial plants and she became famous for her fulsome planting style through her writing. Leaving no areas of bare soil visible was the order of the day, Fish tolerated what some consider 'weeds' if they contributed to the overall effect she sought. Her plant collections ranged from hardy geraniums (cranesbills) to rarer herbaceous plants, some of which she saved from extinction. This garden still reflects the passion of its creator, a gifted amateur gardener.

PAVILION COLOMBE, SAINT BRICE, PARIS, FRANCE
A Hero's Garden

During the First World War, American journalist and writer Edith Wharton set up a network of war-relief organizations, including schools for children fleeing from the war in Belgium and refugee hostels.

Wharton was one of the few journalists and writers allowed onto the front lines. In 1916, she was awarded the Legion d'Honneur for her work. After the war, she moved here and made this garden. Wharton died here in August 1937.

SHAU- UND SICHTUNGSGARTEN HERMANNSHOF, BADEN-WÜRTTEMBERG, GERMANY
A Sustainable Garden

This became one of the most experimental gardens in Europe at the end of the 1970s. A decision was made to follow new principles of planting design developed by plant sociologist Richard Hansen, based on his studies of perennial plants growing in their native habitats – taking an ecological approach.

HEARST CASTLE, CALIFORNIA, USA
The Neptune Pool

Hearst built three swimming pools on this site between 1924 and 1936. Each was bigger than the last.

Hearst Castle sits on the top of *La Cuesta Encantanda* – the Enchanted Hill. The Neptune Pool is one of the most magnificent features that William Randolph Hearst created together with his architect and garden designer Julia Morgan.

Filled with over a million litres (345,000 gallons) of water, its depth varies from 1m (over 3ft) to 3m (10ft). Hearst used to swim in it with the most beloved of his many dachshunds, Helen, and even had a tiny ladder installed in case one of the small dogs fell in.

Before his death on this day in 1951, Hearst was renowned for hosting lavish parties here, where his guests included Charlie Chaplin, Winston Churchill, Greta Garbo and George Bernard Shaw. Visitors today can book swimming sessions in this pool.

HUNTINGTON DESERT GARDEN, HUNTINGTON BOTANICAL GARDENS, CALIFORNIA, USA
An Arid Garden

An otherworldly landscape at Huntington Desert Garden.

When railway magnate Henry Huntington bought this site in 1903, it was a working ranch. His horticultural superintendent Dr. William Hertrich persuaded him to develop the many plant collections that form Huntington Botanical Gardens today.

The Desert Garden's 2,000 species show the full variety of plants that have adapted to thrive in arid conditions. Notables include chunky golden barrel cactus (*Echinocactus grusonii*) grown from seed planted just over 100 years ago, and the tall boojum tree (*Fouqueria columnaris*), given its common name as it was thought to resemble Lewis Carroll's fantasy creation in *The Hunting of the Snark*.

GRACELAND MANSION, MEMPHIS, TENNESSEE, USA
The King's Garden

Elvis poses in front of his custom Music Gates, 1957. There is a rumour that the notes come from the sheet music of 'Jailhouse Rock'.

Not many garden owners invite people to write on their garden walls. But Elvis didn't mind fans signing their names and leaving messages on the Wall of Love. He moved into Graceland at 22 years old, and the famous Music Gates were installed just one month later, making a suitably rock 'n' roll entrance. Imagine the number of photos that have been taken here.

Exceptional fame made him a recluse, but Elvis saw this front garden every time he left the building. The King's premature death was on this day in 1977.

THE INN AT DEATH VALLEY, CALIFORNIA, USA
A Desert Oasis Garden

This oasis has a spring-fed swimming pool, a 'town square' with palm trees and a golf course.

Death Valley is the hottest, driest and lowest of the US National Parks. These gardens were originally designed by landscape architect Daniel Hull in the 1920s to integrate the Spanish Mission-style hotel buildings with the grounds around. Originally built for railroad workers, and formerly known as the Furnace Creek Inn, the hotel has been a place to stay for visitors to the unique area since 1930.

The site was chosen to take full advantage of the landscape and access to spring waters that make the gardens possible and supply the inn's pools. This is North America's only real desert oasis. Rare spring rainfalls add carpets of wildflowers to areas of the beautiful natural landscape of Death Valley.

RASHTRAPATI BHAVAN, NEW DELHI, INDIA
Presidential Palace Garden

Water channels divide this garden into a grid of squares, with lotus-shaped fountains at every crossing.

Formerly the Viceroy's Palace, and now the official residence of India's president, Rashtrapati Bhavan was built between 1913 and 1930. Although the palace has many hundreds of rooms, its architect Edwin Lutyens designed it to be both a city centrepiece and a house with a garden. Formal geometry and symmetry underpin his design, as in all of Lutyens's gardens.

Here, the scale matches the building and the principles of Mughal garden design, with the division of space into four quarters – *chahar bagh*.

POMONA SPROUT'S GARDEN
A Hogwart's Horticulturalist

Pomona Sprout
with her students
(Harry, Ron and
Hermione) and
a mandrake –
a sentient plant
that screams
when unearthed.

At Hogwarts School of Wizardry, herbology lessons are given by Professor Pomona Sprout. Her greenhouse is full of plants, both mundane-looking and exotic – some can talk, some can dance and some are extremely dangerous. Sprout is a Hogwarts' graduate who returned to teach at her old school. Even her name is plant based: *pomona* is Latin for apple, seeds sprout when they germinate and 'sprout' is the short name for the not universally loved winter vegetable which is thought to have originated in Belgium.

STOWE LANDSCAPE GARDENS, BUCKINGHAMSHIRE, ENGLAND
Paradise Fields

James Gibbs'
Palladian Bridge
with the folly
tower, Gothic
Temple, in the
distance.

To create this fine landscape garden, generations of the Temple family employed a roll call of leading architects, designers and gardeners, including Lancelot 'Capability' Brown early on in his career. The original village of Stowe was moved over the 17th and 18th centuries to make way for this area of the garden, known as the Elysian Fields. Elysium was a paradise afterworld in Greek mythology.

Winding paths reveal perfect views that show the skills of those who planned them centuries ago. There are many historic garden buildings here, more than at any other garden in the country. Classical allusions and political references can be 'read' or the magnificent landscape can simply be enjoyed.

GARDENSTOWN, ABERDEENSHIRE, SCOTLAND
The Garden at Seatown

This garden has to be simply planted as it faces the full force of sea storms!

Confusingly, Gardenstown is a fishing village on the Moray Firth. It was given its name in 1721 by the laird, Alexander Garden. The original village is built on a series of terraces cut into the hillside and includes part of Main Street midway down the hill, and some of the houses on Seatown at the bottom. The narrow roadway between Seatown and the water was constructed in the 1940s. Before this, access was via the footpaths that run up and down the hillside. Some pass small gardens including this one, made in the last 25 years. Simply and sparingly planted, it is the perfect place to enjoy stunning sunsets and spot the occasional dolphin.

DELIUS IN HIS GARDEN AT GREZ-SUR-LOING (EARLY 1900S), JELKA ROSEN
A Composer Among the Flowers

Delius in his Garden at Grez-sur-Loing (painting, early 1900s) by Jelka Rosen. The garden was large and very beautiful, sloping down to the bank of the River Loing.

German artist Jelka Rosen was the wife of composer Frederick Delius. They lived at Grez-sur-Loing, in north-central France from 1897 until Delius's death in 1934. Their garden inspired both Rosen's painting and her husband's musical compositions, in particular the orchestral work 'In a Summer Garden' (1908).

Percy Grainger (see page 20) became a friend and suggested Delius write shorter works for orchestra, resulting in the nature-inspired 'On Hearing the First Cuckoo in Spring' and 'Summer Night on the River'.

DUMBARTON OAKS, WASHINGTON DC, USA
A Conference Garden

Dumbarton Oaks
Research Library
and Collection
supports
scholarship
in Byzantine
studies, Pre-
Columbian
studies... and
garden design.

American landscape architect Beatrix Farrand worked on this garden for the owners Mildred and Robert Woods Bliss for nearly 30 years. Farrand was one of the first American women to qualify in this field. Her designs followed the advice of her mentor Charles Sprague Sargent, director of the Arnold Arboretum, Boston – 'to make the plan fit the ground and not twist the ground to fit the plan'.

Dumbarton Oaks is a fine example of Farrand's work. Her design transformed a former farm on a sloping site into an elegant garden that sits easily in the surrounding landscape. It became a research institute, library and garden of Harvard University in 1940. Four years later, between 21st August and 7st October, a meeting was held at Dumbarton Oaks with representatives from China, the Soviet Union, the USA and the UK, which established proposals for a world organization that formed the basis for the United Nations.

THE HOUSE OF THE GOLDEN BRACELET, POMPEII, ITALY
A Roman Garden Fresco

This fresco covered the wall of an open-plan living room. It faced a real garden and so gave the illusion of a much larger garden space.

Vesuvius is thought to have erupted on this day in 79 CE and buried this wall painting under volcanic debris for many centuries. Knowledge of what Roman gardens looked like was expanded when beautiful frescos like this were finally uncovered in the early 20th century.

The House of the Golden Bracelet shows the Romans' love of garden greenery, water in different forms, ornaments, statues, colourful flowers and birds such as the barn swallow, rockdove, magpie, sparrow and golden oriole. This garden was a place of leisure and gave pleasure to the occupants of the house to which it belonged.

The event that destroyed a sophisticated city and many of its citizens ultimately preserved a precious record of their lives.

LAS POZAS, XILITLA, MEXICO
Surrealism in the Jungle

This structure is called 'The Bamboo Palace' or 'Tower of Hope'. It reminds visitors of walking amongst the ruins of an ancient civilization.

Las Pozas is the unique creation of 20th-century poet Edward James. He was a committed surrealist, interested in the fleeting and random; dreams and the subconscious inspired his creativity. This mysterious collection of elaborate buildings, columns, multi-level pavilions, and stairways to somewhere and nowhere was created on land high up in Mexico's subtropical rainforest that James purchased in 1944.

Absent for long periods, his friend and administrator Plutarco Gastélum supervised the teams building the vision in James's mind – there was no masterplan. Today, dripping natural waterfalls and encroaching vegetation degrade the concrete structures. Eventually, this garden will return to the jungle.

SWISS COTTAGE, OSBORNE HOUSE, ISLE OF WIGHT, ENGLAND
A Child's Private Garden

Above: Each of the royal children had a bed in which to grow and tend plants.

Opposite top: *Dahlias, Garden at Petit Gennevilliers* (oil on canvas, 1893), Gustave Caillebotte.

Opposite bottom: *The Fair Toxophilites* (oil on canvas, 1872), William Powell Frith.

Born on this day in 1819, Queen Victoria's beloved consort Prince Albert had the Swiss Cottage built so that the royal children could experience doing ordinary adult tasks of housework and gardening. Each child had a plot to tend with scaled-down gardening tools and their own monogrammed wheelbarrow. Beds were planted with a mixture of edible plants and flowers. Produce was assessed by the head gardener; if it met his standards, Prince Albert paid market rates to the child who had grown the crop.

Tucked away from the main house, it is a truly private world.

DAHLIAS, GARDEN AT PETIT GENNEVILLIERS (1893), GUSTAVE CAILLEBOTTE
An Impressionist Garden

French artist Gustave Caillebotte was also a skilled gardener, like his close friend Claude Monet. A leading Impressionist, he painted in a more realistic style than many of his peers. Caillebotte frequently painted all aspects of his own garden. Here, his prized dahlias take centre stage, and perspective underlines the importance of the shaded greenhouse to the serious gardener.

THE FAIR TOXOPHILITES (1872), WILLIAM POWELL FRITH
A Sporting Garden

Interest in archery revived in the 19th century, making it a suitable sport to be played in gardens with mown lawns. This painting shows archery was deemed a socially acceptable garden activity for women. Their clothing made no concession to exercise and ruled out wearing quivers, so arrows were held and picked up by others.

ELTHAM PALACE, LONDON, ENGLAND
Garden Parties

This garden combines historic elements such as a moat with 1930s design.

Eltham Palace has seen centuries of entertaining inside and out. A medieval hall with historic royal connections survived to the 1930s, when it was bought by Stephen and Virginia Courtauld, who transformed the site with an Art Deco house.

The gardens they created are the same mixture of old and new, including a pergola of salvaged 18th-century columns and a sunken rose garden accessed by a bridge over the moat. This garden was the scene of lavish parties in the 1930s, sometimes with live music and fireworks lasting into the early hours, which caused complaints from the neighbours.

DONNELL GARDEN (EL NOVILLERO), SONOMA, CALIFORNIA, USA
Gardens (and Pools) are for People

The pursuit of happiness and well-being lies at the core of this garden.

Unusually, this swimming pool was built before the house it belongs to. The pool was started in 1947 and is key to the landscaped garden masterpiece by renowned American landscape architect Thomas Church. Church was influenced by modernist artists and sculptors, in particular the work of Finnish designer Alvar Aalto (see page 282). It marked a move away from traditional landscape design based on formal axes to new ideas for spaces that reflected the requirements of modern life.

Church's approach was based on the site, the architecture of the house and his clients' preferences, personalities and the practicalities required by their lifestyles, which he explained in his influential book *Gardens are for People* (see page 262). For Church, who died on this day in 1978, gardens really were for people – spaces to enjoy every day, rather than somewhere requiring large amounts of time spent on maintenance.

THE GARDEN LAWN
Mowing the Grass

The arrival of the mechanical mower made lawn cutting a simpler job that did not require additional labour. The machine allowed the development of games designed to be played on garden lawns: croquet became very popular, followed later by lawn tennis.

English inventor Edwin Beard Budding invented the world's first mowing machine. He was inspired by watching a rotary cutting machine remove the nap from quality woollen cloth at a mill near Stroud, Gloucestershire. The 48-cm (19-in) wrought iron framed reel-type mower he produced with partner John Ferrabee, was granted a British patent on this day in 1830.

Before this, lawns were cut by teams using scythes, and sheep kept grass trimmed in large landscape gardens. One of the first mechanical mowers went to the Zoological Gardens at Regent's Park, London; the machine was able to do the work of 6–8 men using scythes and brooms. After Budding's death in 1846, lawn-mower development was taken up by others, including Amariah Hills of Connecticut, USA. Steam-powered mowers were not patented until 1893 by James Sumner of Lancashire.

CARNATION, LILY, LILY, ROSE (1885–6), JOHN SINGER SARGENT
An Evening Glow

Carnation, Lily, Lily, Rose (oil on canvas, 1885–6), John Singer Sargent.

The garden depicted here was located in the Cotswolds village of Broadway, where an enclave of artists, illustrators and craftspeople established themselves in the late 1880s. The artist John Singer Sargent had moved to Broadway and the girls seen in the painting were the daughters of fellow American illustrator Frank Barnard. The unusual title is a line of a popular song, as well as naming the flowers in bloom. Painting took a number of weeks in late August and early September, spread over two years, as Sargent worked when daylight dwindled to capture the glow from the lit Chinese lanterns.

RUTH BANCROFT GARDEN, WALNUT CREEK, CALIFORNIA, USA
Dry Gardens Can be Colourful

This photograph, taken towards the end of her life, shows Ruth Bancroft sitting alongside a giant agave. She died on 26th November 2017, at the impressive age of 109.

Born in Boston on this day in 1908, Ruth Bancroft was a keen gardener and avid plant collector. She made a fine garden that included a collection of irises, but became captivated by succulents in the late 1950s. She grew these in pots in every available space as her collection expanded to include cacti.

In the early 1970s, Bancroft decided to create a new garden using only those plants that are naturally suited to the climate of northern California – warm, dry summers and mild winters with around 50cm (20in) of rainfall. She was ahead of the curve in her ecological approach and conserving water use, and gardened well into old age. Her garden was instrumental in the founding of the Garden Conservancy, whose mission is the preservation of significant American private gardens, open to the public for leisure and as educational resources.

JAMES HITCHMOUGH'S GARDEN, SHEFFIELD, ENGLAND
A Garden that Ebbs and Flows

The view of the greenhouse and path leading towards the house. James Hitchmough's garden boasts successions of colourful blooms throughout the months.

James Hitchmough's approach to planting is based on research and observing plants in their native habitats on his global botanical travels. He is well known for his large-scale planting, notably the Olympic Park in London, co-designed with his colleague at Sheffield University Nigel Dunnett and garden designer Sarah Price.

Hitchmough's own garden shows how his approach works in a small space. The planting includes many South African species, and is designed to ebb and flow through the year, with good ground cover for many months – even in the cooler climate of South Yorkshire.

249

SEETHING LANE, CITY OF LONDON, ENGLAND
Samuel Pepys's Garden

Above: This bust was created by Karin Jonzen in 1983.

Opposite: The majesty of this garden is best seen from the air!

Samuel Pepys lived and worked at the Navy Office on Seething Lane and wrote much of his famous diaries there. On 4th September 1666, as the Great Fire of London raged, Pepys buried 'parmazan cheese', wine and other unspecified items in his garden. His neighbours also buried things that they valued.

A bust of Pepys takes centre stage in this recently revamped garden. Paving stones are carved with significant events from his life – including the burying of his cheese and wine.

CHÂTEAU DE VAUX-LE-VICOMTE, MAINCY, FRANCE
The Precursor to Versailles

Finance minister to King Louis XIV, Nicholas Fouquet commissioned the young André Le Nôtre to design this garden to match his opulent new home in 1650. The moated building appears to float above the 3-km (1.8-mi) long central axis.

Le Nôtre's mastery of design techniques and perspective conceals changes in level from a distance; pools appear uniform in shape but are narrower near the house. The intricate embroidered parterre – *parterre de broderie* – displays immaculate horticultural control, a signature feature of French period gardens.

When Louis XIV saw this garden, he commissioned Le Nôtre to design the gardens at Versailles; he followed his father as principal royal gardener. Fouquet was later convicted for embezzlement.

THE IMPERIAL MOUNTAIN RESORT, CHENGDE, HEBEI, CHINA
A Garden to Avoid the Heat

Visitors can enjoy a boat ride on the lakes. The lakes have been used for pleasure boating for hundreds of years.

As its name indicates, this site was chosen by the Imperial Court for its cooler summer climate. A 10 km (6 mile) long wall was built to enclose the vast park, and many buildings were designed and built to take advantage of views of the lakes, mountains and forested slopes. Development of the garden began in 1703 in the Qing dynasty and successive emperors added to the numerous scenes that were made to replicate landscapes and gardens in other parts of China, including the Jin Shan Garden in Beijing and the Surging Waves Garden in Suzhou.

This is a landscape garden on a grand scale, a combination of lakes, different garden areas and buildings, from pavilions to ornate temples. Many visitors elect to use the electric buses to get around the large state-owned site, which was made a World Heritage Site in 1994.

PLEASURE GARDENS, FESTIVAL OF BRITAIN, 1951
A Centenary Celebration

The front cover of The Guide to Festival of Britain Pleasure Gardens, 1951.

The Festival of Britain Pleasure Gardens hoisted the 'flag of fun' over Battersea Park for six months in 1951. The festival was held to celebrate the 100-year anniversary of the Great Exhibition, in addition to its aim to boost post-war revival. With a fun fair, Peter Pan Railway, a fountain tower topped with an illuminated pineapple alongside a Grand Vista and lawn and flower gardens, there was something for everyone. The large project team included John Piper, Osbert Lancaster and Russell Page, who designed the landscape and gardens.

The festival continued the tradition of earlier pleasure gardens at Vauxhall (see page 300) and Ranelagh (see page 311), but at the same time was forward-looking.

BALMORAL CASTLE GARDENS, ABERDEENSHIRE, SCOTLAND
A Royal Scottish Garden

This photograph of Balmoral Castle and its grounds was taken in 1893.

The private home of the royal family in Scotland, Balmoral was a favourite place of the late Queen Elizabeth II. Prince Albert found the castle in 1852, and for Queen Victoria it was a paradise. They started creating a garden around the castle and every monarch since has left their mark with additions. Herbaceous borders near the house are planted to peak between August and October, traditionally when the royal family are in residence. The rest of the garden blends with the surrounding majestic landscape of the Highlands.

MINE OWN BACK GARDEN (1887), EDWARD ATKINSON HORNEL
A Garden in Light

Mine Own Back Garden (oil on canvas, 1887), Edward Atkinson Hornel.

Scottish artist Edward Atkinson Hornel was a keen gardener. He was closely associated with the group of artists known as the Glasgow Boys, who liked to capture the naturalistic effects of light on contemporary scenes, including figures in the landscape. Bold brush strokes give garden soil a freshly dug appearance and kale, which is usually picked during September, looks ready to harvest in this early work. Bright flecks and a timber arch show a garden that is both beautiful and productive. After this painting, Hornel travelled to Japan, which influenced his work and his later garden at Broughton House, Kirkudbright.

THE FLOATING GARDENS, TOWER BRIDGE MOORINGS, LONDON, ENGLAND
Garden Barge Square

Several of the 30 floating barges, on which about 70 people live.

London's only floating gardens were devised by architects Nick Lacey & Partners. The collection of once-redundant barges began with a single vessel in the 1990s. They bring green to the riverside and increase the types of habitats that support a wider range of wildlife. The barge planting includes quince trees, lavender and herbs. Box hedging makes another surprisingly formal addition.

Garden barges are part of the moorings' infrastructure, connected by metal brows specifically designed to follow the tidal flow. Beneath the gardens, living and studio spaces look up through skylights to the greenery.

NATIONAL SEPTEMBER 11 MEMORIAL, NEW YORK CITY, USA
The 9/11 Remembrance Garden

This garden is a place of remembrance and the contemplation of loss.

These two voids outline the lost twin towers and honour victims of the attacks on the Pentagon, at Shanksville, Pennsylvania and at the World Trade Center on both 11th September 2001 and 26th February 1993. Michael Arad's concept of the central voids is titled *Reflecting Absence*. Landscape architect Peter Walker designed the masterplan for the symbolic landscape that links with Arad's voids. A Memorial Grove comprises hundreds of swamp white oak trees, while the Glade is a gathering space where the name of every victim is read out each 11th September. Victims' names are inscribed on the bronze plaques around each void, where four-sided waterfalls are ever-flowing into a central abyss.

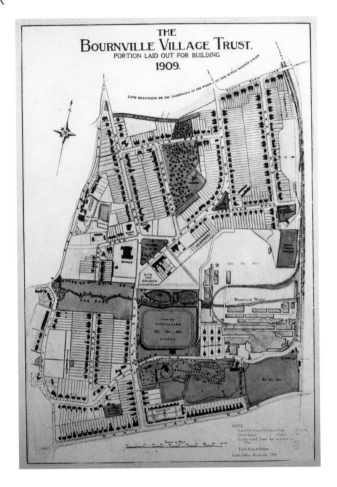

BOURNVILLE, BIRMINGHAM, ENGLAND
Chocolate-Box Gardens

A plan for the garden village from 1909.

In 1879, George and Richard Cadbury moved their chocolate and cocoa factory from the city of Birmingham to what was then a rural area and named it Bournville. It was dubbed the 'factory in a garden'; more land was purchased, and a model village planned comprising well-constructed homes with large gardens, initially for key workers.

Cadbury set rules on garden size, and each was to be planted with at least six fruit trees on the basis that this would encourage workers to grow their own fruit and vegetables. A village council and residents' associations were set up early on and the estate expanded. The Bournville Village Trust still exists today.

THE ROALD DAHL MUSEUM AND STORY CENTRE, GREAT MISSENDEN, BUCKINGHAMSHIRE, ENGLAND
The BFG (Big Friendly Garden)

The exterior of the writing shed in its original location in the garden of Gipsy House, Great Missenden.

When he found it hard to concentrate on his writing in his busy family home, Cardiff-born Roald Dahl was inspired by a solution devised by fellow Welsh writer Dylan Thomas (see page 178). The dimensions and roof of Dahl's yellow-doored brick version match those of the hut belonging to the poet, but it has fewer, smaller windows, and Dahl sometimes wrote under a lamp with the curtains closed, sitting in an armchair. He kept a collection of objects that inspired him on his desk.

Dahl, born on this day in 1916, wrote many of his famous stories here including *Matilda* and *Charlie and the Chocolate Factory*. It is said he told his children there were wolves inside the hut to stop them from disturbing him! The interior of the hut was moved from the garden of his home, Gipsy House, to the nearby museum in 2011.

TWO WOMEN IN A GARDEN (C.1933), ERIC RAVILIOUS
Garden Companionship

*T*wo *Women in a Garden* is an early work by Eric Ravilious, who has become one of Britain's most popular artists. This garden is at Brick House, Great Bardfield, Essex, the home of fellow artist Edward Bawden, where Ravilious and his wife Tirzah lived for a while. She is shelling peas while Bawden's wife Charlotte sits reading in a deckchair. Ravilious rarely painted family and friends in his pictures.

15TH SEPTEMBER

POTENT PLANTS GARDEN, TORQUAY, ENGLAND
A Murder Mystery Garden

*T*he Potent Plants Garden in Torre Abbey Museum, Torquay, celebrates the author Agatha Christie (see page 278), the town's best-known resident. Christie used knowledge gained through her pharmacy training in the First World War in her books. She learned which plants are deadly and which are poisonous but have medicinal use in the correct dosage, which informed the methods used by the villains in her novels. This garden shows the beauty of these plants.

Above: The
process of making
floating gardens
in the lake of
Xochimilcho
created canals.

Opposite top: *Two
Women in a Garden*
(watercolour,
c.1933), Eric
Ravilious

Opposite bottom:
Every plant in this
garden is featured
in an Agatha
Christie story
or has another
connection with
the Queen of
Crime.

THE FLOATING GARDENS OF XOCHIMILCHO, MEXICO CITY, MEXICO
Aztec Canal Gardens

Thousands of acres of floating gardens – *chinampas* – were made by
the Aztecs as spaces to grow crops for their capital city Tenochtitlán,
sited on an island in the crater lake of an extinct volcano. The Spanish were
overwhelmed by the scale of these growing gardens when they saw them.
Chinampas are ecosystems created by hand, making a network of canals
in the process. A proportion are still in use today for flower and vegetable
growing near what is now Mexico City. It is a popular area to visit, bright
flowers matched by colourful flat-bottomed boats – *trajineras* – adding to
the festive atmosphere.

Mexico achieved independence from the Spanish on this day in 1810.

261

GARDENS ARE FOR PEOPLE (1955), THOMAS CHURCH
Garden Philosophy

The cover of the first edition of *Gardens are for People* (1955).

Renowned American landscape architect Thomas Church believed in giving his clients what they wanted from their gardens, designing them to suit the lives of all the people who would live in them. His book *Gardens are for People* looks at the garden as a place for outdoor living rather than primarily concerned with horticulture. It makes garden design relevant to modern life. Church presents case studies of garden design solutions for a range of different size plots in a witty, conversational style. Advice on dimensions of features and scale never dates. His approach was very influential among other landscape architects and garden designers. Gardens are for people ... to enjoy.

RANGER'S HOUSE, GREENWICH, LONDON, ENGLAND
The Bridgertons' Front Garden

Ranger's House, shown here without the artificial wisteria that is added for filming.

Fans of the popular TV series *Bridgerton* will recognize this house and its front garden as the London home of the Bridgerton family. But in reality, it is the Ranger's House, located on the edge of Greenwich Park, rather than its supposed address in central Mayfair.

At the time the *Bridgerton* drama unfolds, this Georgian house belonged to Augusta, Duchess of Brunswick, the elder sister of George III. It ceased to be a private residence in 1898; a few years later London County Council took ownership, and the grounds were turned into a bowling green and tennis courts. Now it is an English Heritage property, with a classically simple front garden, and the unique Wernher Collection of artworks and jewellery is displayed inside the house.

ZANDRA RHODES' GARDEN, LONDON, ENGLAND
A Colourful City Garden

The famous designer's hair matches the *Rosa Mexicano* on her garden walls and furniture. Rhodes was born on this day in 1940.

The coloured walls of this city rooftop garden reflect its owner Zandra Rhodes' legendary love of colour. But these bright shades were actually chosen by renowned Mexican architect Ricardo Legoreta when he designed the Fashion and Textile Museum below – established by Rhodes in 2003. The shade of pink is known as *Rosa Mexicano* and is commonly seen in all aspects of Mexican life, as are the contrasting shades of blue and orange, although these colours have a different intensity in the subdued London light. Planting is in a range of containers, boosted in summer months when indoor pot plants are brought outside. This garden shows the link between nature, colour and fashion.

FEDERAL RESERVE BOARD GARDENS, WASHINGTON DC, USA
The New American Garden

Ornamental grasses and a spirited fountain feature in the garden of the central bank.

Renovating this public garden on top of the Federal Reserve's underground car park in the centre of Washington DC was a big break for landscape architects Wolfgang Oehme and James van Sweden, the latter of whom died on this day in 2013. Earlier planting of trees and shrubs had been decimated by severe winter weather.

Oehme and van Sweden's 1977 design drew inspiration from the Great Plains and prairies of the USA. Bold drifts of herbaceous plants combined with swathes of ornamental grasses around sheltered seating created the first New American Garden. It was a pioneering approach to the design and planting of both public and private gardens.

ABBOTSFORD, MELROSE, SCOTLAND
Sir Walter Scott's Garden

Abbotsford
opened to the
public just five
months after
Scott's death on
this day in 1832.

Known for works including *Ivanhoe* (1819) and *The Lady of the Lake* (1810), Sir Walter Scott became a best-selling author while living in the original farmhouse on this site. With lead architect William Atkinson, his wealth enabled him to build his vision of an ideal home. Abbotsford set the fashion for the Scots Baronial style of architecture, a complete contrast to Georgian symmetry.

He created this garden with advice from architects and friends to set off his home. A Regency layout of three garden rooms links the building with the natural landscape of the estate. The South Court's colonnade wall hints of monastic origins and has a wealth of architectural details that allude to historical events. In Scott's time, the Morris Garden was a high-walled sunken flower garden; stone steps still lead to a fine viewpoint. The walled kitchen garden is the largest room; a conservatory designed by Scott survives in a flower-filled garden.

PATRICK LEIGH FERMOR GARDEN, KARDAMYLI, GREECE
A Mediterranean Garden

Patrick and Joan Leigh Fermor at home in Kardamyli.

British travel writer Patrick Leigh Fermor discovered Greece's Mani peninsula in the early 1960s. He and his wife Joan decided to make their home here and this was where he wrote some of the travel books that made his name. Steeped in mythology, the area retains an isolated, other-worldly quality. The couple stayed in the nearby village while the house was built. Everything had to be brought to site by mule; villagers donated local limestone rocks. Garden terraces are true outdoor rooms with timeless panoramic views to the sea; some are shaded by stone colonnaded porches or timber beams, with pebble mosaics set into paving and low walls to sit on. For several decades from the 1970s onwards, Leigh Fermor and his wife drew many other artists and intellectuals to this beautiful setting above the Mediterranean Sea.

KNOLL GARDENS AND NURSERY, WIMBORNE, DORSET, ENGLAND
A Wildlife Haven

Knoll Gardens boasts beautiful and colourful grasses in Autumn.

This garden feels much larger than it is, but retains an intimate atmosphere. Paths wind through many different informally planted areas, the space shaped by mature specimen trees, shrubs and a water garden. Since 1994, Neil Lucas and his team have turned the former private botanic garden – known as Wimborne Botanic Garden – into a naturalistic garden that is a haven for wildlife. Lucas is a renowned expert on ornamental grasses and author of *Designing With Grasses*. This garden shows to full effect the varieties that can suit all underlying conditions and how to combine them with suitable perennials – an excellent additional display for its nursery.

THE BUTCHART GARDENS, VICTORIA, VANCOUVER ISLAND, CANADA
A Quarry Garden

The walls of the densely planted Sunken Garden are covered in grasses and mosses, but you can still see the shape of the original quarry.

It is hard to believe that these plant-filled gardens – one of the most visited in North America – were made in a limestone quarry, exhausted of raw materials needed for the family cement business. In 1912, Jennie Butchart began to repair the site by bringing in many tonnes of topsoil. She created a series of garden areas in the ravaged space and devised suitable ways to green the quarry's rock face sides – now the Sunken Garden. Butchart expanded the gardens and visitors were always welcomed. Many of the ground level beds are packed with masses of colourful plants that require high levels of maintenance and changing out several times a season. The gardens remain family-run and were made a National Historic Site of Canada in 2004. Visitors are embraced by this garden of lush green foliage and colourful flowers – Jennie Butchart's vision.

THE LOST GARDENS OF HELIGAN, CORNWALL, ENGLAND
Lost and Found Garden

Moisture-loving ferns, trees and plants surround a pond in the Tropical Jungle Garden at The Lost Gardens of Heligan.

Uncovering this lost garden was a huge feat of horticultural archaeology. Heligan declined into a bramble- and ivy-entwined secret lost garden at the start of the First World War in 1914 when its gardeners enlisted. As with those of other large estates, many never returned.

Born on this day in 1954, businessman Tim Smit discovered the gardens in 1990, and led the project to bring them back to life. Staff say some areas are haunted and avoid being alone in them. There is still an air of mystery and romance about Heligan, despite its revivification.

HIGHCLERE CASTLE, BERKSHIRE, ENGLAND
The Real Downton Abbey

The Monk's Garden in the grounds of Highclere Castle.

Highclere Castle has become synonymous with the fictional stately home of *Downton Abbey*. Its state rooms were the rich backdrop to family drama; the approach through its parkland heralded the start of every episode of the TV series, first broadcast on this day in 2010.

The view to the castle is reminiscent of the Houses of Parliament, as both were designed by the same architect, Sir Charles Barry. Tucked away in Highclere's 'Capability' Brown landscape lies the Monk's Garden, reflecting the historic origins of the estate when it was granted to the Bishops of Winchester in 749 CE.

THE GARDEN OF THE HESPERIDES (C.1870–73), EDWARD BURNE-JONES
A Garden for Gods

The Garden of the Hesperides by Edward Burne-Jones shows three goddesses dressed in robes of sunset colours dancing around a tree of Golden Apples, its trunk entwined with a serpent.

In Greek mythology, the Hesperides were nymphs, or minor goddesses thought to embody elements of the physical world. Daughters of Hesperus, they represented evening and sunsets. Their role was as guardians and to tend the Garden of Hera, the queen of the gods.

This sacred place was the famed home of the Golden Apples, said to give sunsets their golden hues. It was also a safe place to store the powerful tools of the gods, including Hades' helmet or cap of invisibility, Athena's shield and the winged sandals of Hermes. The Hesperides were supported as custodians of these valuable items by a 100-headed dragon, Ladon. The garden's location was secret, but with other mythology and the fact that the sun sets in the west suggest a setting to the west of Greece, possibly in the Atlas Mountains. Victorian artist Edward Burne-Jones was interested in classical mythology and painted this subject several times.

LACOCK ABBEY, WILTSHIRE, ENGLAND
The First Photographed Garden

Above: One of Fox Talbot's photographs of Lacock Abbey featured in *The Pencil of Nature* (1844–46).

Right: The 1835 photographic negative of one of the abbey's windows.

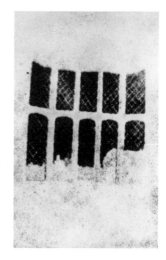

Former resident of Lacock Abbey, William Henry Fox Talbot, was a pioneer of Victorian photography. In 1835, he created the earliest surviving photographic negative of a small window in the abbey's South Gallery. Previously, a fixed image could only be created by painting or drawing, and his discovery also meant multiple prints could be made.

The earliest garden photographs in the UK were taken at Lacock Abbey. Fox Talbot's book *The Pencil of Nature* (1844–46) was the first mass-produced book featuring photographic illustrations.

VILLA ADRIANA, TIVOLI, ITALY
Hadrian's Garden

The Canopus of Villa Adriana (or 'Hadrian's Villa') was a pool that represented a branch of the Nile in Egypt.

Emperor Hadrian is thought to have designed this garden himself at the beginning of the 2nd century CE. It reflects his great interest in art and architecture. Full advantage was taken of the site; the garden layout retains views out to the surrounding countryside. Hadrian drew inspiration from the classical sites and landmarks he had seen on his travels through parts of the Roman Empire, including the remains of a peristyle (colonnaded) garden adopted from Greece. Overall, features are linked by strong axes. Hadrian loved his villa and its garden, and their remaining ruins are an enduring legacy to this love.

PALM HOUSE, ROYAL BOTANIC GARDENS, KEW, LONDON, ENGLAND
Kew Gardens

An engraving of the Palm House at Kew from a book printed in 1851.

When it opened in 1848, the Palm House was the first glasshouse built on this scale. To achieve its distinctive curvilinear shape, architect Decimus Burton, born on this day in 1800, and engineer Richard Turner, borrowed certain shipbuilding techniques. It was built to accommodate exotic palms and tender plants that were being discovered and brought back from around the world.

It is an indoor rainforest, a living laboratory. At first plants were kept in pots and displayed on shelves, with the more efficient bed system adopted in the 1860s. Rainforests cover just 2 per cent of the world's surface, but are home to 50 per cent of plant species. The Palm House now houses plants from the most threatened habitats on Earth. Planting includes ancient cycads, medicinal plants and the Madagascan palm, also named the suicide palm as it lives for around 50 years, flowers once and then dies soon after.

ZHOU ZHENG YUAN, SUZHOU, CHINA
The Humble Administrator's Garden

One of the garden's 48 beautiful buildings overlooks water. Suzhou was praised by the explorer and merchant Marco Polo as the "Venice of the East".

This is one of the finest gardens in China, created in the 16th century by a retired tax collector, Wang Xian Chen. The classical Chinese strolling garden has central elements of water and decorative garden buildings connected by a network of twisting paths. Numerous fine views are framed by portals, moon gates and windows. After Wang's death, his son ran up large gambling debts, which forced him to sell the garden. It was later sold several more times and split into three sections. In 1949, the Chinese government rejoined the sections, and opened the restored garden to the public. The People's Republic of China celebrates its National Day on 1st October.

CAMBRIDGE UNIVERSITY BOTANIC GARDEN, CAMBRIDGE, ENGLAND
A University Garden

Planting outside the Cambridge University Botanic Garden's glasshouses. They contain everything from delicate alpines to arid-loving cacti and succulents.

John Stevens Henslow, a professor of botany at Cambridge from 1825 to 1861, was instrumental in moving the garden, which had been founded in 1762 on another site, to its current location. It was designed to display a great tree collection with sinuous paths through woodland. Henslow was a mentor to his student Charles Darwin and drew inspiration on theories on variation and the nature of plant species from his famous student. The eastern part of the garden remained undeveloped until a bequest from horticulturalist Reginald Cory in 1834; work began in 1951.

Today, this garden has cutting-edge laboratories and beautiful planting outside. But the garden's heart lies in its herbarium comprising 1 million plants collected from across the world; plant specimens are dried, prepared and notated. This collection includes plants collected by Darwin on the *Beagle* voyage (1831–6).

GREENWAY, GALMPTON, DEVON, ENGLAND
Agatha Christie's Garden

A glimpse at the
house through the
woodland setting
of the banks of
the River Dart.

Agatha Christie bought Greenway in 1938 when she had achieved
success as a best-selling author of crime fiction. It was a secluded
holiday and weekend retreat, known to her since childhood. The library
here has copies of all her published works, but she wrote at her other house,
Styles, in Sunningdale.

The woodland garden was an inspiration and source of pride to the
Queen of Crime. Greenway appeared in a number of her books under
different names. In 2013, it was the location for the 'Dead Man's Folly'
episode of ITV's *Agatha Christie's Poirot*.

The garden played a significant role as one route winds through it to
the crime scene – a boat house overlooking the River Dart. A tranquil
backdrop to murder, its meandering paths and clearings made good places
to stimulate Poirot's 'little grey cells'.

ADACHI MUSEUM OF ART, YASUGI, JAPAN
Living Work of Art Garden

The Pond Garden
at Adachi
Museum of Art.
The building is
the *Seifu* teahouse
which is meant
for enjoying
Sencha, or
green tea.

Adachi Museum of Art was created by Adachi Zenko in 1970. Born locally, he rose from humble beginnings to achieve great success in wholesaling textiles and real estate.

The museum houses his large collection of Japanese art, including many paintings by Yokoyama Taikan, and he designed the gardens as a living work of art. Museum windows frame views out into the beautiful gardens so they appear as large paintings, and artworks are rotated in line with the seasons. It is regularly named as one of the best gardens in Japan.

WOOLSTHORPE MANOR, LINCOLNSHIRE, ENGLAND
Isaac Newton's Apple Tree

Newton's famous apple tree still stands in front of the house, continuing to bear fruit in Autumn. Its variety is 'Flower of Kent'.

Isaac Newton returned to his family home in 1665 when studies at Cambridge University were interrupted for several years by an outbreak of the plague. This is a significant garden, whether the legend of the falling apple that led to his discovery of gravity is true or not. Newton's theory of gravity applies to the universe: he established a new approach to science, where theories were tested and proved through observable experiments. Newton's ability to explain complex theories in relatively simple laws was pioneering.

Over 300 years later, a hand-drawn image that showed Newton sitting under the apple tree became the first logo of Apple Computer Company.

VILLA SAVOYE, POISSY, FRANCE
Designed by Le Corbusier

A living room looks out onto a courtyard with raised beds.

'The house is a machine for living in.'

LE CORBUSIER

Villa Savoye shows how Swiss-French architect Le Corbusier, born on this day in 1887, combined essential garden elements of light and space with his designs. Built in 1931, the modernist house and garden are entwined, indoor space in balance with outside courtyards. Walls that extend into the garden from the building have 'window' openings, large doors make for good indoor/outdoor flow. A wall projects upwards to the roof terrace making it a sheltered, private sunbathing place among raised beds of planting. This is certainly more a garden than a machine.

VILLA MAIREA, NOORMARKKU, FINLAND
A Garden of Curves and Lines

The house is in an L-shape, with the pool and lawn in the angle of the L.

Villa Mairea is a classic of 20th-century architecture. Finnish architect Alvar Aalto was commissioned by the owners of a leading timber company, Harry and Maire Gullichsen, to design their summer house in 1938.

In a small woodland clearing, the garden combines classical straight lines with modern curves in an asymmetric design. The organically shaped pool and angular decking adjoining the terrace were groundbreaking. Aalto is also famous for designing the 'Savoy' glass vase (1936), which resembles this pool, and curving bentwood furniture.

GRESGARTH HALL, CATON, LANCASTER, ENGLAND
An Award-Winning Garden

Morning dew adds an extra touch to the magic of the garden at Gresgarth Hall.

Renowned designer Arabella Lennox-Boyd first began creating this garden in 1978. A difficult site, with its steep valley setting in an area with harsh weather, it has a sense of light and a tranquil atmosphere. Formal terraces around the house and garden areas defined by different types of planting relax into naturalistic spaces and an arboretum of rare trees and large shrubs.

This garden is considered by many to be one of the finest in the UK and in 2020 it won the Judges Choice Award at the Historic Houses Garden of the Year.

MENDIPS, LIVERPOOL, ENGLAND
John Lennon's Childhood Garden

John Lennon's aunt Mimi was very proud of her house and garden.

Born on this day in 1940, John Lennon was living at Mendips with his aunt and uncle when he met Paul McCartney (see page 15), an event that proved to be the start of a revolution in popular music. His mother was a frequent visitor. Tragically, she was killed while crossing the road after visiting her sister.

In the early days, Lennon's band practised in the cramped front porch as his aunt did not appreciate the noise. Later they used the front room in McCartney's home at Forthlin Road while his father was out.

Lennon's aunt Mimi sold the house and moved away in 1965. In 2002, Lennon's widow Yoko Ono bought the property, and donated it to the National Trust.

FIGURES IN A GARDEN (C.1935), FRANCIS BACON
An Unusual Landscape

Bacon's *Figures in a Garden* shows a strange figure partly obscured by tree branches, while a dog-like creature paws at it.

This painting by Irish-British artist Francis Bacon was first displayed under this title in 1937, at an exhibition of Young British Painters. It is rare for two reasons: it has survived when the artist destroyed many works from this period; and landscape was not one of his usual subjects.

The ambiguity of the painting's meaning is heightened by the fact that on several occasions it was exhibited with different titles including *Seated Figure*, *The Fox and The Grapes* and *Göring and his Lion Cub*. But it was not uncommon for Bacon to give his works different titles, and he had regular sessions of either destroying his paintings or reworking them. Gardens are also subject to destruction and revamping, whether they are prompted by natural events, fresh inspiration or changes in ownership.

PEPYS HOUSE, BRAMPTON, CAMBRIDGESHIRE, ENGLAND
Buried Treasure Garden

Pepys described the landscape around his garden as 'the largest and most flowery spot the sun ever beheld'.

Pepys House was the family home of Samuel Pepys, and he referred to it often in his famous diaries. He sent his father and wife Elizabeth to bury his valuables in the garden here in June 1667, after the Dutch fleet sailed up the Thames. The valuables were buried in haste in the kitchen garden, and when Pepys went to retrieve them after the threat of invasion was past several months later, he had great trouble finding the unmarked location.

Pepys's diary entries detail the eventual successful recovery of his gold, on this day in 1667. But despite this account, the removal of a garden wall nearly 200 years later revealed an iron pot containing silver coins – small change – from the same period.

Gardens have been places for burying treasure for many centuries. Several lucky UK garden owners discovered buried treasure in their gardens during lockdown – some while simply weeding, with no metal detectors required.

DENMANS GARDEN, FONTWELL, WEST SUSSEX, ENGLAND
Glorious Disarray Meets the Grid

Denmans is a garden for people to enjoy in all seasons, with plenty of quiet corners.

Joyce Robinson started to make this garden in 1946. Her book *Glorious Disarray: The Creation of a Garden* details her years of garden-making. Her naturalistic planting style was underpinned by a good structure of trees and shrubs. She first introduced gravel to the garden in 1970 – long before others in the UK – after seeing how well plants grew in stony ground on a visit to the Greek island of Delos.

Having met Robinson at the garden previously, landscape designer John Brookes (see page 131) moved into Denmans' old stable block, renovated and renamed it the Clock House, and started his garden design school in 1981. He took over the whole garden when Robinson retired. Under his care and direction, it became a teaching resource demonstrating his approach to garden design using a method he called the 'grid'. Denmans has no formal axes leading to focal points, few straight lines and traditional paths.

HUMMELO, THE NETHERLANDS
Piet Oudolf's Garden

Perrenials and grasses make this garden beautiful in Autumn. Oudolf's planting style looks natural but everything has its place.

Piet Oudolf's own garden began as part of a plant nursery for his garden design practice. As the season progresses, its clipped hedges and trimmed shapes of evergreens visually recede against the massed plantings of perennials and ornamental grasses that have become his signature planting style.

Plant structure and shape are central to Oudolf's work and a year-round constant. Colour ebbs and flows from early summer to autumn. Retention of seedheads, spent flowers and foliage are highlighted by winter frosts.

THE ALNWICK GARDEN, NORTHUMBERLAND, ENGLAND
Contemporary Pleasure Garden

The first feature to greet visitors is the cascade, which performs choreographed water displays every half an hour.

The Duchess of Northumberland made a bold decision to create a new garden at the centre of a 'Capability Brown' landscape. Opened on this day in 2001, this grand cascade welcomes visitors right at the garden's entrance. Designed by Wirtz International, Belgium (see page 98), father Jacques and son Peter created a contemporary feature based on classic elements.

A series of terraced steps form weirs that send water cascading down the slope, with regularly changing flow rates further enlivening the feature. Spaces in the undulating clipped hornbeam hedge allow visitors to appreciate the effects.

But this is just the start of the pleasure to be had at Alnwick. Take the sinuous path to the walled garden with its large plant collections, pergolas, arbours and water rills. Further exploration reveals quieter, secret spaces – even in this very popular garden.

LA LOUVE, LUBERON, FRANCE
An Hermès Tapestry

Above: The garden has been maintained according to its original design.

Opposite top: Piet Oudolf's typical perennials and grasses in Chicago (see page 288).

Opposite bottom: Bosco Verticale has inspired similar structures around the world.

Born in 1916, Nicole de Vésian created this garden after she retired at 70 from a successful career as a textile designer at Hermès. A life in Paris was swapped for a neglected house on a steep, stony hillside in Bonnieux, and the rest of her life was spent restoring her home and creating this inspirational garden. She chose plants that were suited to the harsh conditions. Early on, a limited budget prompted her to buy frost burnt cypresses from a local nursery and trim their unsightly tops flat to encourage fresh side growth. Her balance of plant forms and well-placed groupings create tapestry effects. But it is her masterly hand-trimming of plants that adds a distinctive quality, inspired by the naturally mounded shapes of native plants in the landscape that enable their survival through drought and destructive Mistral winds.

LURIE GARDEN, MILLENNIUM PARK, CHICAGO, ILLINOIS, USA

An Urban Prairie

This naturalistic garden in a corner of Chicago's Millennium Park brings dynamic, prairie-style planting to the centre of the city. The masterplan by Gustafson Guthrie Nichol with planting design by Piet Oudolf was finished in 2004. Four seasons of colour and texture of perennial plants and grasses against the urban backdrop has evolved over the years.

BOSCO VERTICALE, MILAN, ITALY

Modern Hanging Gardens

Architect Stefano Boeri collaborated with botanists Emanuela Borio and Laura Gatti to take city reforestation to new heights. Opened on 17th October 2014 after over five years of construction, *Bosco Verticale* ('Vertical Forest') comprises two towers of apartments in the Isola neighbourhood of Milan, with balconies planted with 900 trees, some up to 9m (around 30ft) high.

HEVER CASTLE, EDENBRIDGE, KENT, ENGLAND
A Classical Sculpture Garden

Hever Castle's Italian Garden, with some of its large sculpture collection.

The garden at Hever was created between 1904 and 1908, primarily to house William Waldorf Astor's large collection of Italian sculptures and antiquities. Constructed by landscape company Joseph Cheal and Son, 1,000 men worked on implementing the design, and about 800 of them spent two years excavating the 14.2-ha (38-ac) lake alone. Classical formal gardens and naturalistic landscape areas were constructed and planted on 50ha (125ac) of former marshland in just four years – an incredible feat. This garden is only now reaching maturity. The Italian Garden is a particular highlight, the perfect setting for Astor's fine collection of Greek and Roman statues, and the Loggia is a place to reflect on the results of the efforts of the many men who laboured to create this magnificent garden.

Astor, who died on this day in 1919, emigrated to England in 1890; Cliveden (see page 194) was another home in his property portfolio. Hever Castle was once the childhood home of Anne Boleyn.

TRENGWAINTON, CORNWALL, ENGLAND
A Garden with Scarecrows

One of the many scarecrows made by schoolchildren and volunteers at Trengwainton annually.

Some large gardens hold annual exhibitions and competitions that involve local schools and the community. In 2022 at Trengwainton, Cornwall, the theme of the scarecrow exhibition in the walled kitchen garden, which ran from August until October, was 'When I grow up, I want to be ...' Around 60 children from local schools made 13 scarecrows, aided by creative workshops run by artist John Keys and volunteers from the garden.

The diversity of scarecrow characters included an RNLI volunteer captured in mid-rescue hanging from a winch, a footballer kicking a ball, and an artist painting a picture. Placed in the five distinct sections of the walled garden, visitors were able to vote for their favourite.

Trengwainton's walled garden was built in the 1820s by Sir Rose Price to the same overall dimensions as Noah's Ark, as given in the Bible – 50 × 300 cubits, or 23 × 135m (74 × 443ft).

LOWTHER CASTLE GARDENS, PENRITH, CUMBRIA, ENGLAND
The Garden in the Ruins

Climbing plants partially clothe stone walls, while naturalistic perennial planting defines paths through the space. This garden has a new life.

Lowther Castle had a room for every day of the year, with fine, expansive gardens to match. Hugh Lowther, 5th Earl of Lonsdale, unexpectedly inherited the title at 25 years old, together with the estate and two London mansions. He was a great sportsman – he established boxing's Lonsdale Belt award – but he was also extravagant and squandered his fortune in 60 years. The castle and gardens were abandoned in 1936 and lawns were concreted over for wartime use by tank regiments. In 1957, the castle was demolished, leaving only its façade and the outer walls. The gardens became a wilderness, home only to chickens, pigs and bats.

Garden designer Dan Pearson drew up a 20-year masterplan after a decision to revive the gardens was taken in 2008. The garden inside the walls is partly inspired by other ruins reclaimed by nature and the Garden of Ninfa near Rome in Italy.

ABERFAN MEMORIAL GARDEN, ABERFAN, WALES
A Memorial Garden 2

The Aberfan
Memorial Garden
has benches for
reflection.

This garden stands on the site of the former Pantglas Junior School in Aberfan. It commemorates the 116 children and 28 adults who died in the Aberfan Disaster, when a colliery spoil tip collapsed and engulfed the school at 9.13 a.m. on this day in 1966.

It is an important place of remembrance for the bereaved families, survivors, the whole community and for visitors to pay their respects to those who lost their lives.

THE HANNAH PESCHAR SCULPTURE GARDEN, OCKLEY, SURREY, ENGLAND

A Sculpture Garden

This garden has been a living fusion of art and nature for over 40 years. Before Hannah Peschar and her husband, renowned landscape designer Anthony Paul, arrived here in the 1970s, it was a neglected part of the Leith Vale Estate. Mature trees were retained, and Paul planted beneath them with a restricted choice of plants with architectural habit and leaf shapes. Three naturalistic ponds were added, the surrounding areas filled with swathes of suitable moisture-loving plants; a variety of grasses are used throughout the garden. Carefully curated sculptures are given considered placement against the backdrop of beautiful planting. This garden was one of the first of its kind in the UK, a true work of art.

SAIHO-JI, KYOTO, JAPAN
The Moss Garden

Above: Moss
bridges connect
woodland spaces
at Saiho-ji.

Opposite: The
garden was home
to these 'Swaying
Horses' by Alison
Berman in 2014.
They are made
from fibreglass
and resin.

Famed for its moss garden, Saiho-ji is also known as Kokedera – Moss Temple. The temple building is also covered in moss. Its history stretches back over 1,200 years.

The woodland floor is thickly carpeted with hundreds of varieties of moss in a range of different depths of pile or plant heights. Moss is a beautiful natural ground-cover plant for woodland, not just an unwanted weed to be banished from lawns.

FRIAR PARK, HENLEY, OXFORDSHIRE, ENGLAND
George Harrison's Garden

George Harrison sits in his garden on the artwork of the record sleeve *All Things Must Pass* (1972).

This garden has had two moments of fame. The lawyer and microscopist Sir Frank Crisp created fantastic gardens based on the look and feel of a monastery's garden. Working with landscape designer Henry Milner, the extensive gardens included a fine rock garden surmounted by a scale version of the Matterhorn, complete with snowy slopes of crushed white stone. It was regularly open to the public soon after it was finished in 1898 and very popular with visitors.

After Crisp's death in 1919, the garden declined under subsequent owners. Friar Park was saved from demolition when George Harrison bought the property in 1970. He became a keen gardener at a time when gardening was not a usual pursuit for a rock star; home and garden were escapes from fame. The cover of his first solo album, *All Things Must Pass* (1972) shows Harrison in his garden with some of the large gnomes that were uncovered. Dressing to match them shows his droll humour. His autobiography *I Me Mine* was dedicated to 'gardeners everywhere'.

WARLEY PLACE, ESSEX, ENGLAND
Miss Willmott's Ghostly Garden

Today, the garden at Warley Place is a nature reserve, with occasional remaining glimpses of its former glory.

At the height of its fame, the garden at Warley Place had fantastic plant collections and was tended by 100 gardeners. It was the creation of Ellen Willmott, a gifted, wealthy, self-taught horticulturalist, remembered by the many plant species and cultivars named 'Miss Willmott' or 'Warley'.

In 1897, Willmott was one of two women to be awarded the inaugural Royal Horticultural Society's Victoria Medal of Honour. Gertrude Jekyll was the other and came to the presentation, but it remains a mystery why Willmott did not attend.

Miss Willmott's Ghost is the common name for *Eryngium giganteum*, bestowed either because the stories of her sowing its seeds in gardens she visited were true, or because it matches her prickly personality.

The garden at Warley Place fell into decline as her wealth diminished due to her extravagant gardening and the house was demolished after her death.

VAUXHALL PLEASURE GARDENS, LONDON, ENGLAND
London's First Pleasure Garden

Vauxhall Pleasure Gardens in full swing, as shown by Thomas Rowlandson in 1809. This illustration was originally published in Ackermann's *Microcosm of London*.

Vauxhall was London's first commercial pleasure garden. Established in 1729 by Jonathan Tyers, the site had been a place for gathering and refreshments visited by people such as Samuel Pepys since the 1660s. Admission to the new garden was one shilling, intended to keep out undesirables, including pickpockets and prostitutes. A place of fashion and culture, Vauxhall exhibited artists such as William Hogarth, making it an early public art gallery. Music by famous composers was performed, including George Frideric Handel; at the height of his fame he became almost a resident composer. But this garden developed a reputation for louche behaviour; dark corners of its shrubberies were ideal for dubious assignations and fancy dress masquerades became notorious for scandalous behaviour. It was a garden for having the best of times, but also a place for behaving badly, and closed for the last time in 1859.

MOUNT STEWART, NEWTOWNARDS, NORTHERN IRELAND
A Whimsical Garden

The Dodo Terrace features all sorts of fun sculptures… but dodos take centre stage.

A sense of fun shines through this most beautiful of gardens. Created in the early 20th century within an existing historic landscape by Edith, Lady Londonderry, wife of the 7th Marquis. Her initial impressions were not good when she first saw the house and garden in 1917, but she went on to make a deeply personal garden that reflects her personality, sense of humour and passion for plants. Formal gardens near the house include an Italian Garden with figures from Greek mythology. The Dodo Terrace is named after concrete sculptures of the extinct bird created by Thomas Beattie. These stand proud of plants and other animals from the 'Ark', which featured in weekly gatherings of the owners' friends during the First World War. Further away from the house, richly planted informal gardens include many rare and tender shrubs.

HEDGEHOG HIGHWAYS
A Route for Small Creatures

The dramatic decline in the UK's hedgehog population over the last 50 years has accelerated in recent times to the point where the species *Erinaceus europaeus* faces extinction. But the nocturnal animals are welcome wildlife garden visitors, as their diet favours a host of garden pests, including slugs and snails. Garden owners can help the natural roamers by cutting small holes in the bottom of boundary fences. A series of 13 × 13cm (5 × 5in) square – or rounded – archways between gardens create a hedgehog highway to safe food supplies and shelter for hibernation, but are too small for most family pets.

Dale Road in Keyworth, Nottinghamshire, was awarded the 2022 title of Britain's Biggest Hedgehog Street, run by the charity of that name. Thirty gardens are linked by 42 highways comprising many gates and tunnels under fences and walls; night-time activity at food and water stations is watched through wildlife cameras set up nearby. This project helps bring diverse communities of people together united in a common cause.

JEALOUSY IN THE GARDEN (1929), EDVARD MUNCH
Disturbing Garden

Above: This version of Munch's *Jealousy* has four characters, instead of his usual three.

Opposite: A 'hedgehog highway' has been created in this garden wall. This one might be large enough for family pets to escape.

Edvard Munch painted 11 works titled *Jealousy* in a period of just over 30 years. This one is at the Munch Museum in Oslo, Norway, and was completed around 1929. The artist suffered from anxiety and depression, and his paintings express complex emotions.

The first *Jealousy* painting featured an Adam and Eve theme that Munch returned to several times in the series. *Jealousy* usually involves three people, but the relationship between characters here is unclear. The faceless man is unsettling, and the foreground character shows the isolation of powerful, perhaps overwhelming, negative emotions. This painting is especially disturbing because being in a garden is widely held to improve mood, induce contentment and provide a sense of well-being.

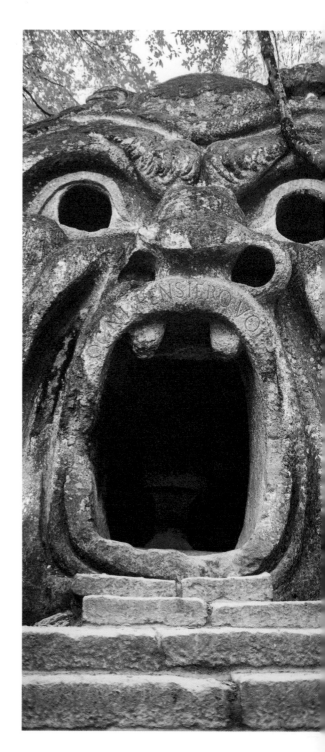

SACRO BOSCO (GARDEN OF BOMARZO), VILLA ORSINI, LAZIO, ITALY
The Park of the Monsters

This garden is also known as Parco dei Mostri – Park of the Monsters. But the Latin *monstrare* means 'to show' or 'to demonstrate'. Each of the garden's surreal monsters, beasts and stone features represents an element of a lost love of its creator Pier Francesco Orsini, Duke of Bomarzo.

The design of this late 16th-century allegorical garden is attributed to Pirro Ligorio, who died on this day in 1583, and it is in complete contrast to other great gardens of that era. After Orsini's death, it was neglected until the 1970s, when the owners began a restoration programme.

BLENHEIM PALACE, WOODSTOCK, OXFORDSHIRE, ENGLAND
A Spooky Garden

Above: Illuminated giant spiders' webs add a ghostly touch to the garden at Blenheim for Halloween.

Opposite: Timeworn steps give a monstrous gaping jaw a strange allure, an invitation to explore the depths within.

Halloween, the Eve of All Hallows, takes its name from the Christian feast of All Saints, a three-day festival that ends with All Souls' Day. It coincides with the Celtic festival of Samhain in which people would wear different costumes and light bonfires to ward off ghosts.

At this time of year, Blenheim Palace's famous gardens are transformed into mysterious haunted woodlands, full of creepy surprises, and its classic historic features become backdrops to ghostly figures. Glowing pumpkins, flickering fires and lighting effects add to the atmosphere of this garden seen after dark as the seasons change.

CASA AZUL, MEXICO CITY, MEXICO
The Day of The Dead Garden

Above: Day of the Dead *ofrenda* with marigolds in the courtyard garden of Frida Kahlo Museum, Mexico City.

Opposite: Monet's water lilies line the base of this shallow pool. They shimmer through clear water viewed from a raised walkway above.

This enclosed small courtyard garden was Frida Kahlo's home, known as Casa Azul (the Blue House) because of the intense colour of the building. It is now a museum that reflects the interests and inspirations of Kahlo and her husband, the muralist Diego Rivera.

El Dia de los Muertos, the Day of the Dead, is a celebration of life and remembrance in Mexico. It is usually celebrated on 1st or 2nd November. Aztec in origin, in Mexico it is celebrated with colourful, elaborate costumes, sugar *calaveras* – skulls – and *calacas* – skeletons, butterflies and marigolds representing light. At Casa Azul, an *ofrenda* or offering for Kahlo is placed on the Aztec-style pyramid structure, built to display the artists' collection of pre-Hispanic art, and the garden is decorated with many pots of bright marigolds – *Tagetes erecta*. Nature and plants were constant inspirations for Kahlo. The vibrant space reflects her art and Mexican culture.

GARDEN OF FINE ARTS, KYOTO, JAPAN
An Open-Air Museum

Tadao Ando is a self-taught architect. Pursuing an earlier career as a boxer enabled him to travel the world and experience different styles of architecture. He designed this space as an open-air museum, displaying full-scale ceramic copies of artworks by world-famous artists.

This sleek, contemporary garden presents Monet's famous water lilies as the base of a shallow pool. They shimmer in clear water viewed from above – a uniquely different view of a very familiar artwork.

COVENT GARDEN, LONDON, ENGLAND
The People's Piazza

This oil painting by Samuel Scott (c.1755) shows the commotion of the market in action less than a century after the Great Fire.

Early records from around 1200 show that this area of fields and orchards was owned by Westminster Abbey, hence the origins of its name meaning 'the garden of the Abbey and the Convent'. Title to the land was granted to the 1st Earl of Bedford in 1552; in the 17th century, it was transformed by the 4th Earl during the first-ever exercise in urban planning. With royal assent, he commissioned the leading architect of the day, Inigo Jones, to create the first public square in the country – the Piazza.

Wealthy families, many with titles, moved into the houses built on arcaded sides to the north and east. After the Great Fire of 1666, the land in the centre evolved into London's largest market, trading in fruit and vegetables. The neoclassical Market Building was built in the mid-19th century. A hundred years later, the market needed more space, and in 1974 it moved out to Nine Elms. Covent Garden has had periods of being fashionable or notorious, but it has long been a vibrant neighbourhood.

20 MARESFIELD GARDENS, HAMPSTEAD, LONDON, ENGLAND
Sigmund Freud's Garden

Freud in the garden with his two grandsons Stephan and Lucian (see page 283), 1938. Today the building is the site of London's Freud Museum.

'Flowers are restful to look at. They have neither emotions nor conflicts.'
SIGMUND FREUD

Freud was a neurologist, inventor and developer of psychoanalysis, and author of the groundbreaking *Interpretation of Dreams* (1900). He and his wife Anna arrived in London in 1938 as refugees from Austria. The garden of their house in Hampstead was appreciated by both, as their former home in Vienna was an apartment.

On 6th May 1939 the weather was fine enough for a party in the garden to celebrate Freud's 83rd birthday, which proved to be his last. As his health deteriorated, Freud's bed was moved to his study facing the French windows that looked out on the garden. While he only lived here for a short time, the garden played a significant part in the final months of Freud's life.

NOVEMBER 5TH (1933), ERIC RAVILIOUS
Bonfire Night

Eric Ravilious captures shared (and separate) joy in a row of small back gardens.

This depiction of people celebrating Guy Fawkes' failed gunpowder plot of 1605 was painted by British artist Eric Ravilious in 1933. It captures a period when many domestic back gardens saw families gathering around bonfires to let off fireworks on this night of the year. Celebrating the 5th of November at home has declined with the decrease in garden size, tighter regulation of the sale and use of fireworks and restrictions in the burning of garden bonfires. But organized public bonfires and firework displays are safer, bring communities together and raise funds for charitable causes.

RANELAGH GARDENS, CHELSEA, LONDON, ENGLAND
The Fun-Fair Prototype

This hand-coloured etching by Thomas Bowles shows people enjoying the area around the Chinese-style Pavilion and Rotunda in 1754.

Ranelagh Gardens were public pleasure gardens built by a syndicate in 1742 on a site of a mansion owned by Earl Ranelagh, to the south-east of the Royal Hospital, Chelsea. A rotunda building inspired by the Roman Pantheon was the centrepiece. The 61-m (200-ft) wide arena with central fireplace held a performance space for orchestras, an organ and featured candle-lit boxes for taking refreshments around its walls. The gardens opened for concerts in 1742, with an admission price of one shilling, and events took place several days a week.

After the initial popularity wore off, attractions were added to the grounds including formal gardens, a canal with Chinese-style pavilion and a summerhouse. Illuminations, magic lanterns and firework displays made night-time visits a magical experience. Subsequently the gardens developed a louche reputation, popularity dwindled and they were demolished in 1805.

DOWN THE GARDEN PATH (1931), BEVERLY NICHOLS
A Garden Book

Beverley Nichols sits in his Surrey garden, 1980.

This book is author Beverley Nichols' witty chronical of attempting to make his ideal garden in the early 1930s. Although it is a period piece, there is a timeless quality to its humour in the face of gardening disasters. It is interwoven with a strong thread of useful, non-garden thoughts, including keeping a sense of perspective and not letting obsessions gain the upper hand. It remains one of the best-loved garden books.

STUDLEY ROYAL AND FOUNTAINS ABBEY, RIPON, NORTH YORKSHIRE, ENGLAND
A Water Garden

The Temple of Piety, which overlooks the Moon Ponds at Studley Royal, was constructed in the 1730s.

One of the finest water gardens in the country, Studley Royal is a subtle composition of a canal, formal-shaped pools and a lake set within a valley. A series of garden buildings on the sloping valley sides provide focal points for vistas carefully composed by the garden's creator, John Aislabie. A former chancellor of the exchequer, his career ended due to his involvement in the South Sea Bubble, an early financial scandal. Aislabie retired to his estate in 1722 and spent the next 20 years, until his death, making this beautiful garden that adjoins the ruins of Fountains Abbey.

BERKELEY SQUARE, MAYFAIR, LONDON, ENGLAND
A Lively Square

Scottish artist Peter Graham captures the buzz of Berkeley Square in his painting *The Nightingale Sang* (2023).

Berkeley Square is one of London's largest and most famous squares and was designed by architect William Kent – although its shape is not a true square. Kent designed the house at No. 44, which remains and is a listed building, and he is also well-known for the landscape gardens he created, including Rousham (see page 201).

As the title of this painting (*The Nightingale Sang*) shows, the square is famous for the song 'A Nightingale Sang in Berkeley Square'. It is not possible to hear nightingales here today, but the sentimental song has been recorded by many famous singers, including Nat King Cole, Bing Crosby, Vera Lynn and Frank Sinatra. London plane trees (*Platanus × acerifolia*) shading the public space are among the oldest and highest-value trees in the city, as calculated in a recent survey.

THE BLOEDEL RESERVE, BAINBRIDGE ISLAND, WASHINGTON, USA
The Japanese Garden

Dark conifers and moss covered ground stand-out against the warm autumnal colours of acers.

This nature reserve was the private home of Prentice Bloedel and his wife Virginia. The reluctant heir of a thriving timber business, Bloedel was an early and committed environmentalist, and worked with several renowned landscape architects and designers, including Thomas Church and Richard Haag, to shape a series of gardens requiring as little intervention as possible.

The Japanese Garden was designed by Fujitaro Kubota. Curving paths invite a stroll through contrasting areas including traditional rock and gravel gardens. The Bloedels gifted the reserve to the community, and it opened to the public in 1988.

'BLOOD SWEPT LANDS AND SEAS OF RED' (2014), PAUL CUMMINS AND TOM PIPER
We Will Remember Them

Ceramic poppies bleed out of the Tower across the moat. In the distance volunteers continue to add poppies.

From 1914 to 1918, the fields of Flanders in Belgium were sites of major battles and turned into seemingly barren land. But in early summer swathes of bright red poppies – *Papaver rhoeas* – flowered among fallen soldiers and the detritus of war. The power of Canadian physician John McCrae's poem 'In Flanders Fields' (1915) established a link between the poppy and remembrance of those who had died in battle. This link was taken up by chairman of the Royal British Legion Field Marshall Douglas Haig in 1921, and artificial poppies were made to commemorate Armistice Day, later named Remembrance Day, on 11th November.

In this public commemoration of the centenary of the First World War, each of the 888,246 ceramic poppies in the moat of the Tower of London represents a fallen member of the British or Colonial services. It took thousands of people several months to install this visually powerful work.

STOURHEAD, WILTSHIRE, ENGLAND
A Garden for Strolling

Autumnal colours frame the Pantheon, Palladian Bridge and lake at Stourhead.

Stourhead is one of the finest English landscape gardens. Created between 1741 and 1780 by Henry Hoare II and open from the earliest times it remains true to its first description as a 'living work of art.' An expansive lake is a centrepiece that reflects a magnificent collection of garden buildings and mature rare trees. Vistas and views are revealed while strolling the garden's winding paths. Hoare's vision is heightened in autumn, when trees and shrubs are burnished with seasonal warm colours.

THE ARTIST'S GARDEN AT GIVERNY (1900), CLAUDE MONET
A Garden in Art

The Artist's Garden at Giverny (oil on canvas, 1900), Claude Monet

A garden photograph captures a single moment; a garden painting explores colours, shapes, textures and the relationship of each element to another. Monet thought his garden was his greatest work of art. It was like a giant organic palette. Plant colours and shapes were ordered in the way he viewed and wanted to paint them. His preferences may differ from horticultural purists.

Monet led the Impressionist artists in painting out of doors – *en plein air* – to capture the effects of different light levels, seasons and weather. He painted his garden constantly.

This painting helps us to experience how Monet saw this part of his garden when the irises were in full flower.

CLAUDE MONET'S HOME AND GARDEN, GIVERNY, FRANCE
A Garden as Art

Monet in his gardens at Giverny in 1925, just under a year before his death on 5 December 1926. He was born on the 14 November 1840.

Claude Monet was passionate about plants. As mentioned opposite, he considered his garden at Giverny to be his greatest work of art and he developed the garden throughout the time he lived at Giverny. Monet appears here in gardening mode. He personally supervised all aspects of making his garden, from the sowing of seed to deciding which trees to remove when he started on its development.

The Clos Normand – enclosed flower garden – was the view of the garden from the house and studio. Seeing the garden and its creator in black and white highlights the nuances of plant shape and texture. When plants are in full growth the straight lines of the borders here are masked with foliage and flowers. With no colour to distract, the power of using a simple band of nasturtiums at the front of the borders is clearly shown.

MUSEUM OF MODERN ART ROOF GARDEN, NEW YORK CITY, USA
High Rise, Low Maintenance

American landscape architect Ken Smith designed this garden to disguise the roof of the new extension to the Museum of Modern Art, designed by architect Yoshio Taniguchi. Opened in 2005, the appearance of a giant, military-style camouflage transforms the roof into a visible garden space, like an abstract work of art. Here, recycled rubber chips, crushed glass, crushed marble, artificial large rocks and artificial plants make a modern work of garden art.

AUTUMN (1950), EDWARD BAWDEN
A Garden Print

Edward Bawden was an artist, printmaker, illustrator and a keen gardener. This lino cut may be a study of Bawden's own garden at Brick House, Essex, where he established an artistic hub, and where other artists, such as Eric Ravilious, also lived for a while.

This garden view emphasizes the abundance of autumn and suggests the ongoing gardening tasks of getting ready for the season ahead.

RHS GARDEN BRIDGEWATER, SALFORD, MANCHESTER, ENGLAND
Old Ground, New Garden

Above: A fountain in the Paradise Garden, designed by Tom Stuart-Smith.

Opposite top: The rooftop functions as a piece of art only visible from neighbouring high-rises.

Opposite bottom: *Autumn* (lino-cut/print), Edward Bawden

RHS Bridgewater, the Royal Horticultural Society's fifth and newest garden, opened in 2021 after a year's delay due to the Covid pandemic. One of the largest garden projects in Europe in recent years, it took four years to create on the former site of Worsley New Hall, demolished in 1940. The garden's master plan reflects the heritage of earlier grand formal gardens. The Weston Walled Garden was one of the largest in the country; its double walls have been retained, and the inner section divided in two. The Paradise Garden is a fusion of Mediterranean planting and Islamic tradition; the Kitchen Garden reflects local history and heritage in a contemporary layout.

Unusually, the garden's restoration workforce included rare-breed pigs, which proved to be the most efficient and sustainable way of improving the ground in the orchard – they are still kept in the garden along with hens and ducks. The local community were also involved from the early stages.

THE NO DIG GARDEN
Shallow Work

Charles
Dowding's farm
in Shepton
Montague,
Somerset,
England.

'No dig saves time and keeps it simple, so that you can continue cropping all year without using synthetic feeds or poisons.'
CHARLES DOWDING'S SKILLS FOR GROWING

No dig gardening methods mean less maintenance, as without digging, weeding is reduced. Adding organic materials to the soil surface and letting nature do the work of taking nutrients down into the soil also reduces watering. Charles Dowding is one of the UK's leading advocates. Many professionals have adapted versions that minimize soil disturbance and work with existing conditions when planting gardens of all types and size.

HOLKER HALL, CARK-IN-CARTMEL, CUMBRIA, ENGLAND
Garden with Labyrinth

The design of the labyrinth at Holker Hall is in the shape of a yin-yang symbol.

Labyrinths are traditionally an aid to contemplation, with their twisting paths to central points. This one in the wildflower meadow at Holker Hall links the formal gardens with the landscape beyond.

Designed by labyrinth specialist Jim Buchanan with Grania, Lady Cavendish, it combines a pattern of curving paths based on an Indian temple motif with 12 slate monolith stones that resonate with the Cumbrian tradition of stone circles.

THE WINTER GARDENS, BLACKPOOL, ENGLAND
Winter Garden Under Glass 1

The Fernery at Blackpool Winter Gardens as it was in the early 20th century. It shows that the Victorian craze termed Fern Fever – *pteridomania* – remained popular.

Historically, a heated garden glasshouse nurtured exotic plants through freezing winter chill and was also a way to have year-round flowers, depending on the temperature.

Building public glasshouse winter gardens was a way of extending the holiday season at British seaside resorts in the late 19th and early 20th centuries. They were places to take a stroll through glazed floral halls when it was wet or cold outside and provided a much-needed seasonal boost when travel to exotic climes was beyond the means of most. Blackpool's famous Winter Gardens opened in 1878 and included a palatial glass-roofed, plant-filled hall, a Pavilion Hall for special events, and indoor and outdoor skating rinks – these last features meant that winter was not completely denied to Blackpool's visitors.

THE MAZE, HAMPTON COURT PALACE, ENGLAND
A Garden of Twists and Turns

The yew maze at Hampton Court Palace was originally planted in hornbeam.

Hampton Court Palace gardens are large enough to get lost in without entering its famous hedge maze. Fittingly, the exact origins of this maze are also veiled by time, but it is thought to have been started in the last years of William III's reign and completed by his successor Queen Anne's head gardener, Henry Wise. It is not the largest maze at 1,350 m₂ (one-third of an acre) with 800m (half a mile) of paths that twist, turn and dead end. The average time to reach its centre is 30–45 minutes. The maze remains as popular today as it was when the gardens were first opened to the public in 1838.

THE RED HOUSE, ALDEBURGH, SUFFOLK, ENGLAND
Benjamin Britten's Garden

The back garden of the Red House was home to many parties over the years. Today visitors can picnic there.

English composer Benjamin Britten was born on this day in 1913. The house he shared with his partner Peter Pears from 1957 has a large garden around it where guests were entertained, croquet and tennis were played, and vegetables were grown. A formally laid out front garden has simple planting that complements the house. Inside, a large studio was Britten's main work space. Outside, he used a brick and pantile roofed garden shed as a place to compose music towards the end of his life, in addition to his studio inside the house. It is Grade II listed for its history rather than architecture – he wrote *Death in Venice*, *Phaedra* and *Third String Quartet* there.

'TRELLIS' (1862), WILLIAM MORRIS
A Wallpaper Garden 2

This wallpaper also inspired the garden at Morris's home, Red House in south-east London (not the same Red House as seen opposite).

This garden trellis is an early block-printed wallpaper designed by William Morris for his purpose-built home, Red House in Bexleyheath, south-east London, designed by the architect Philip Webb. Morris created the trellis and flower pattern and asked Webb to design the birds as he was a keen ornithologist. Instantly recognizable as typical of Morris & Co.'s style, it references garden trellises and the plants trained on them as seen in illustrations of medieval and Tudor gardens.

RED GARDEN, SYDNEY, AUSTRALIA
The Living Sculpture Garden

This photograph by Jason Busch shows the garden's strong relationship between its landscaping and planting.

This is more a living sculpture than a garden. Designed by Czech landscape architect Vladimir Sitta, and installed by Bates Landscape, it shows elements of earth, fire, air and water that have become a signature of Sitta's work. While plants are not always of prime importance in his gardens, Australian nature is a constant source of inspiration to Sitta. Angular sections of walls built of red rocks from central Australia project upwards, appearing to sculpt the ground. Their colour offsets the pale, paved terrace and sets off sparse planting in this dramatic garden.

EGYPTIAN GARDEN TOMB PAINTING (1350 BCE)
The Ancient Garden

Nebamun's garden was painted on the walls of his tomb so that he could take it to the afterlife. The goddess of the sycamore, surrounded by her produce, is shown in the top right-hand corner.

This tomb painting fragment shows the garden pool of Nebamun, a wealthy Egyptian accountant from the 18th Dynasty. The outer hedge around the water includes date palms and sycamores, while an inner border suggest smaller plants around the pool that is alive with fish and fowl. Ancient Egyptian gardens had three elements still found in many gardens today: a wall or hedge to enclose the site, water – the source of life – and plants. These usually included a mixture of trees producing edible fruit and decorative flowers.

Egyptian gardens were expensive to build as the climate made growing difficult away from the River Nile. Signifiers of status and wealth in life, garden images and models were included in elaborately constructed tombs so that earthly possessions and treasures could accompany the dead into the afterlife.

CRAGSIDE, MORPETH, NORTHUMBERLAND, ENGLAND
Renewable Energy Garden

Cragside's owner Lord William Armstrong, born on this day in 1810, was an industrialist, engineer and innovator. He invented a dynamo to harness the hydroelectric power produced by water from his hillside garden and grounds to generate electricity to light his home. It was the first house in the world to be lit this way.

Some called Cragside the Palace of the Modern Magician. The steep site has magnificent views and Victorian-style gardens, with carpet bedding on terraces, tall conifers underplanted with rhododendrons, ferneries and grottoes.

KARL FOERSTER GARDEN, POTSDAM, GERMANY
The Hair of Mother Earth

Above: Karl
Foerster Garden's
sunken garden,
shown here in
autumn.

Opposite: The
iron bridge over
Debden Burn
to the house at
Cragside.

Karl Foerster, who died on this day in 1970, was an influential nurseryman and pioneering plant breeder who introduced a new approach to planting design. The sunken garden shows his combination of architectural and naturalistic planting styles, developed over nearly 60 years of gardening on this site.

Foerster's particular interest was breeding hardy perennials including asters and delphiniums and observing how combinations of plant communities performed after planting. He is most famous for his use of a wide range of ornamental grasses, that he described as 'the hair of Mother Earth', in his planting schemes. In particular, *Calamagrostis* – reed grass – is linked with his name.

NEMO'S GARDEN, SAVONA, LIGURIA, ITALY
A Garden Below Us

Salads growing 6m (20ft) below the surface of the sea.

This garden was the first to grow terrestrial plants in underwater biospheres. Sergio Gamberini is the founder of a diving-equipment company and a keen gardener. Finding the perfect growing conditions for basil inspired this innovative garden that combines his two passions – scuba diving and gardening.

The project has developed since it began in 2012. Air-filled transparent biospheres are anchored by chains fixed to the seafloor 6m (20ft) below the surface. Plants grow in soil-free mediums, some hydroponically, and are kept moist by water that collects inside the biospheres. Daily care is computer-controlled and the garden is self-sustainable. Plants thrive in these mini greenhouses, protected from temperature extremes, with sunlight filtered by the blue seawater.

INTERNATIONAL SPACE STATION (ISS) GARDEN
A Garden Above Us

Salads growing 400km (250mi) above the surface of the Earth.

The official name of this garden on the International Space Station is the Vegetable Production System, but it is better known as Veggie. Its purpose is to help NASA study plant growth in space and simultaneously add fresh food to the astronauts' diet. In addition to its practical function, the same psychological benefits of gardening on Earth apply in space – happiness and a sense of well-being are both enhanced. Growing plants in a zero-gravity, sealed environment without sunlight becomes increasingly important as space travel extends further. It's gardening, but not as we know it.

DUNROBIN CASTLE, GOLSPIE, SCOTLAND
The Scottish Versailles

Dunrobin Castle gardens under snow. The gardens also feature a falconry with daily falcon displays.

A fitting choice for St. Andrew's Day, Dunrobin Castle is the most northerly of Scotland's great houses, home of the Sutherland family, and was remodelled by architect Sir Charles Barry in 1850. He designed these formal terrace gardens to reflect the French style of the house and was inspired by the parterres of Versailles.

In the castle's long history there have been many dramatic events. A ghost is said to haunt a tower room overlooking this garden. Margaret, daughter of the 14th Earl, was promised in marriage to the son of another earl, but she had already fallen in love with a stable boy. Her father disapproved, banished her love and locked Margaret in the tower. The boy returned to help her escape using a rope to reach the garden; she was hanging onto it when her father discovered them and demanded she climb back up. But Margaret decided she could not live without her true love, let go of the rope and fell to her death. The sound of her crying ghost is said to be heard near the tower.

WOOLBEDING GARDENS, WEST SUSSEX, ENGLAND
A Special Blend Garden

The 10-sided Woolbeding Glasshouse opens up to allow its plants direct access to ventilation and sunlight.

Woolbeding Gardens have been developed over the last 50 years by tenants of the National Trust Stewart Grimshaw and the late Simon Sainsbury. They have worked with a number of renowned designers to add contemporary facets. The Silk Route Garden, a recent addition, features sinuous paths meandering through 12 distinct climate regions of the historic Silk Road and their related 300 plant species. Just beyond the garden wall, a striking kinetic Glasshouse reveals a lotus-shaped flower when its roof is open. It's the result of six years of design, development and planning by Hetherwick Studio to realize Grimshaw's vision. It joins a William Pye water sculpture and neo classical pavilion by Philip Jebb – both created to mark fallen large trees. Herbaceous borders by American designer Lanning Roper and a Pleasure Garden area inspired by 18th-century landscape gardens and designed by Julian and Isobel Bannerman are combined into one harmonious whole at Woolbeding.

2ND DECEMBER

GARDEN SCENE IN SNOW (1854), UTAGAWA HIROSHIGE AND UTAGAWA KUNISADA
A Printed Garden

This scene of a garden under snow is the central part of a triptych that tells the story of Prince Azuma Genji. It shows that snowfall adds another dimension to the beauty of a Japanese garden. Snow accentuates the stone toro – lantern – highlights the sculptural shape of tree trunks and gives the appearance of adding a profusion of blossom to their pruned branches. The azure stream adds a vibrant note to this wintry garden scene.

3RD DECEMBER

THE PEOPLE'S PALACE, GLASGOW, SCOTLAND
Winter Garden Under Glass

Glasgow's Winter Gardens are part of the People's Palace, which opened to the public in 1898. The great glasshouse was used as a music venue, a popular urban public garden space with exotic planting including palm trees. In 1944, the complex became a museum of the city's social history. At time of publication, the Winter Gardens were closed, with complete restoration promised.

GREEN ISLAND GARDENS, COLCHESTER, ESSEX, ENGLAND
The Greene Winter Garden

Above: Hamamelis mollis is the first witch hazel into flower here.

Opposite top: Garden Scene in Snow (woodblock print, 1854), Hiroshige and Kunisada.

Opposite bottom: An aerial photograph of the complex from 2021.

For the latter part of November, December and January, Francis Bacon's calendar to ensure continual garden life advocated planting 'Things as are Greene all Winter' with the few early flowering plants known in the early 17th century. Even before the warmer winters of recent years, there are many early flowering shrubs to enliven winter gardens, including Christmas box (*Sarcococca confusa*), wintersweet (*Chimonanthus praecox*) and witch hazel (*Hamamelis* spp.). Witch hazel's fragrant and curious spider-like flowers borne on bare wood add colour, scent and presence to the winter garden.

Green Island Gardens hold one of the UK's national collection of witch hazels, with around 100 different varieties. Flower colour ranges from burnished copper to red, tangerine to pale yellow; fragrance varies with flower shades from spicy cinnamon notes to sharp citrus scents. Leaves turn to fiery autumn shades before flowering.

5TH DECEMBER

HIDCOTE MANOR GARDEN, GLOUCESTERSHIRE, ENGLAND
A Garden of Rooms

Lawrence Johnston planted miles of different hedges to create this garden of rooms after acquiring Hidcote in 1907. American-born but a naturalized Brit, he was not professionally trained but had a strong sense of design and good planting skills.

In 1948, Hidcote became the first property the National Trust acquired specifically for its garden. In recent years, the garden has returned to Johnston's original vision of a 'wild garden in a formal setting'. One of the most influential 20th-century gardens, it has inspired many gardeners.

Frost on the topiary birds in the White Garden at Hidcote. This garden is said to have inspired Vita Sackville-West at Sissinghurst (see pages 166–7).

BETTY FORD ALPINE GARDENS, VAIL, COLORADO, USA
A Rocky Mountains Garden

The Betty Ford Alpine Garden has the highest elevation for a botanical garden in North America; it is located in Vail, which is better known as a ski resort. Its mission is to promote the conservation of plants adapted to grow above the tree line and fragile mountain environments.

The Rocky Mountains make the perfect backdrop to the range of garden settings that display the variety and beauty of alpine plants.

COLLEGE GARDEN, WESTMINSTER ABBEY, LONDON, ENGLAND
The 900-Year-Old Garden

Hidden behind the walls and buildings of Westminster Abbey precinct, this garden has been cultivated for over 900 years. A wall built in 1376 is the oldest surviving section. Historically, gardener monks grew vegetables, medicinal plants and a few ornamentals, but also had to attend daily services. Today, gardeners carry on these traditions by growing similar plants.

THE SNOWMAN
The Snowman's Garden

Above: A regular 'backyard' in Arizona, USA, after a rare snowfall.

Opposite top: The garden is open for visitors over winter, but the paths are not maintained.

Opposite bottom: College Garden under snow.

The first fall of snow gets people of all ages out into the garden to make snowpeople, the perfect medium for amateur sculptors. It is believed that snowmen were first made to ward off evil winter spirits. An early documented one appears in an illustrated Book of Hours dated 1380, but it may be the artist monks having fun in the margins of the manuscript, as the snowman looks half-melted by sitting near a fire.

Traditional two- or three-ball shapes are simple and fun to make. Historically, pieces of coal were used for eyes and mouth. A sharply pointed nose is a also a worldwide tradition. One of the first snowmen with a carrot nose features in an animated film of 1943 *Der Schneemann* – The Snowman. The transient charater also had a personality that endeared him to viewers.

THE GARDEN VINEYARD, MOOROODUC, VICTORIA, AUSTRALIA
A Fusion Garden

This garden became known internationally after it was featured on Monty Don's BBC series *Around the World in 80 Gardens* in 2008.

Created by Di and Doug Johnson in 1994, the Garden Vineyard combines traditional European design with a modern Australian approach. It is a successful fusion of two styles, from trimmed hedges defining the lawn, clipped sentinels of common lilly pilly (*Syzygium smithii*) adding evergreen structure to a formal garden room, to another distinctive area planted solely with Australian native plants. The view from the terrace of this peaceful garden is across a lawn leading gently down to the vineyard.

HOBBITON™ GARDENS, MATAMATA, NEW ZEALAND
The Lord of the Gardens

The Hobbiton movie set is now a popular tourist destination.

J. R. R. Tolkien's vision of Bag End is set on a real sheep farm surrounded by the beautiful New Zealand landscape. These Hobbit Holes on Bagshot Row were used for both *The Lord of the Rings* and *The Hobbit* film trilogies. Some of the original homes created for the first *Lord of the Rings* location filming in 1999 were left. Ten years later, the number of Hobbit holes increased and were finished in fantastic detail for *The Hobbit*. Brightly painted front doors and pretty cottage gardens add a sense of the familiar while simultaneously being transported to a different world.

HENRY MOORE'S GARDEN AND STUDIO, PERRY GREEN, HERTFORDSHIRE, ENGLAND
Famous Garden Thefts

Henry Moore cast this work, *Reclining Figure*, in 1962. It is situated at the Sainsbury Centre in Norwich, UK.

Who better to place sculptures in gardens and landscapes than the celebrated sculptor who created them? Henry Moore and his wife Irina moved to Perry Green in 1940 after their house in Hampstead was damaged in a bombing raid. The gardens are relatively formal close to house and studio, but become more open with views to the countryside beyond.

Monumental, larger works have permanent sites chosen by Moore, while the display of smaller pieces changes. All sculptures play off the background of garden planting and surrounding rural landscape.

The theft of public sculptures has risen in the last 20 years. Large works by eminent artists are not exempt from this trend. Moore's copy of *Reclining Figure* (1969–70) was displayed at the garden until it was stolen in December 2005. It has never been found. A large work at 3.6m (12ft) long, weighing 2.1 tonnes (over 330 stone), it required a crane to lift it, so the crime was well planned.

344

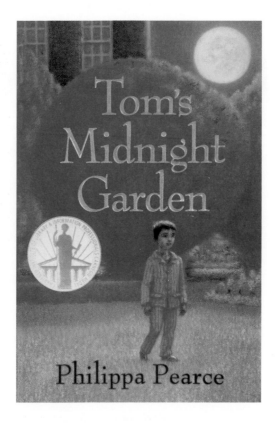

TOM'S MIDNIGHT GARDEN (1958), PHILIPPA PEARCE, ILLUSTRATIONS BY SUSAN EINZIG
A Garden by Moonlight

This front cover is from the 2008 edition of *Tom's Midnight Garden.*

'Every night now Tom slipped downstairs to the garden. At first he used to be afraid that it might not be there. Once, with his hand already upon the garden door to open it, he had turned back, sick with grief at the very thought of absence.'

TOM'S MIDNIGHT GARDEN, CHAPTER 6

Tom is quarantined to his aunt and uncle's house when his brother has measles. Homesick and suffering with insomnia, one night he hears a clock in the communal hallway strike 13. When he investigates, he finds a door that leads into a garden. This is his first sight of a place he has been told does not exist, as his aunt and uncle live in a flat in what used to be an old mansion.

Tom returns every night, enchanted by the garden and the children he meets there. Seasons are reflected in the garden's changed appearance every night. *Tom's Midnight Garden* is a well-crafted story about the power of gardens to affect emotions.

MADISON SQUARE GARDEN, NEW YORK CITY, USA

The Non-Garden Garden

This is the most famous garden without a garden. An alternative definition of a garden in North America is a large public hall. The first 'Garden' at East 23rd and Madison was created by famous showman P. T. Barnum in 1874. After Barnum, the arena changed hands several times. Eventually, renowned architect Stanford White was commissioned to design a Moorish-inspired city showpiece. This second garden achieved notoriety when the architect was shot dead there during a performance.

SHEFFIELD WINTER GARDEN, SHEFFIELD, ENGLAND

Winter Garden Under Glass 3

One of the largest temperate glasshouses to be built in the UK during the last 100 years, this winter garden was part of an inner-city regeneration project. Its parabolic timber structure was formed by the glued laminate process known as 'glulam', using larch from sustainable forests. Smart building management control keeps 2,500 plants from around the world protected year-round.

GONE WITH THE WIND (1939)
The Garden at Tara

Above: Vivien Leigh runs across the garden at Tara.

Opposite top: A photograph of the second Madison Square Garden, taken in 1900.

Opposite bottom: Sheffield Winter Garden's could accommodate 5,000 ordinary domestic garden greenhouses.

The Tara estate plays a central role in *Gone With the Wind*. It's always difficult to portray central characters from bestselling books on film. Landscape architect Florence Yoch recreated this garden from the much-loved bestseller with a limited budget on a Hollywood studio back lot.

Yoch advocated that the garden should have a romantic, softer, less manicured appearance. Her detailed research on the garden plants of Georgia made California plants appear on film like the trees, shrubs and climbing plants of the southern state. The props department's artistry was key. Yoch's private clients included many Hollywood stars and movie moguls.

Gone With the Wind was released in the USA on this day in 1939 and in the UK on 18th April 1940.

THE TALE OF PETER RABBIT (1901), BEATRIX POTTER
Mr McGregor's Garden

This illustration from the 1902 edition of *The Tale of Peter Rabbit* shows Peter Rabbit munching radishes in Mr McGregor's Garden.

Beatrix Potter (see page 168) self-published her first book, *The Tale of Peter Rabbit*, on this day in 1901. It introduced the rabbit and his family's relationship with Mr McGregor and his garden. Peter was based on Potter's childhood pet rabbit, which she walked on a lead. She denied basing McGregor on a real person, but he may be a combination of her mentor on fungi, Charles McIntosh, and onetime landlord, Atholl McGregor.

Peter's mother instructed her offspring not to enter this productive garden because their father was caught by the gardener and met an unfortunate end. His siblings obeyed, but Peter did not. It's unclear if McGregor is protecting his own garden or if he is an employed gardener. Potter's other illustrations show it as a walled garden with a door, box hedged beds, and pond for filling watering cans. Gardeners tend to have varying degrees of tolerance for different wildlife visitors to their gardens.

LAMPORT HALL, NORTHAMPTON, ENGLAND
The First Garden Gnome

Lampy among the snowdrops at Lamport Hall. Warmer winters can see snowdrops bloom as early as December.

Gardener and landowner Charles Isham, born on 16th December 1819, is famous for bringing the first garden gnomes to the UK. They populated his extraordinary rockery, which he built close to the house as he wanted to see it from his bedroom. Construction began in 1847; the rocky structure measured 7.3m (24ft) high, 27m (90ft) long and 14m (47ft) wide. It comprised a miniature landscape of mountains, crevices and intricate caverns that Isham built and planted himself over a 40-year period – gradual development was his intention. His interest in gnomes as German folklore mountain spirits grew, and around 1874 the first miniature china figures began to populate suitable settings within the rockery. After his death, legend has it that his family shot at them with air rifles. Lampy is the sole survivor of his collection and lives inside Lamport Hall. Garden gnomes continue to divide opinion and remain banned from the RHS Chelsea Flower Show.

KENROKU-EN, KANAZAWA, ISHIKAWA, JAPAN
Garden of the Six Sublimities

This garden looks magnificent in the snow. To the top-left of this picture, you can see the majestic *yukitsuri*.

This garden takes its name from the ancient Chinese landscape theory that six essentials are required to make a perfect garden: abundant water, antiquity, artificiality, broad views, seclusion and spaciousness. One of the finest Japanese landscape gardens, Kenroku-en has many flowering trees that change with the seasons.

The iconic Kotoji Toro lantern is the garden's symbol. Its distinctive shape and uneven legs make it stand out. When one of the legs broke it was not repaired but left in a state of imperfect beauty – *wabi sabi*.

A garden for all seasons, winter snow adds another dimension. The garden is renowned for its use of *yukitsuri* – snow hanging – a system of canes and ropes to protect tree branches from collapsing under the weight of the snow.

GADS HILL PLACE, HIGHAM, KENT, ENGLAND
A Flat-pack Christmas Gift

Charles Dickens'
writing studio,
the Swiss Chalet
of Gads Hill,
photographed
in 1906.

Dickens' novel *A Christmas Carol* was first published on this day in 1843. It was written while he was living in Doughty Street, London. He bought and moved to Gads Hill Place in 1856. The Swiss chalet that was to become his writing studio there arrived in 58 boxes at his local railway station in 1864. It was a Christmas gift from his actor-manager friend Charles Fechter, who helped install it in the garden area known as the Wilderness. To access it, Dickens had to walk through a previously built tunnel under the busy road that separates this area from the main garden. The location of the studio ensured his work was uninterrupted.

The tunnel still exists today at Gads Hill Place, but the chalet has been relocated to the garden of Eastgate House – a fine 16th–17th-century building in Rochester that inspired Dickens. It is now a museum of the great Victorian novelist's life and works.

POINSETTIA GARDEN
Flower of the Holy Night

Poinsettias
growing as large
shrubs in a
Mexican garden.

Poinsettias are native to South America and Mexico; to the Aztecs they were a symbol of purity. Their botanical name *Euphorbia pulcherrima* means 'the most beautiful euphorbia'. The common name is derived from Joel Roberts Poinsett, the first American ambassador to Mexico in 1825. He was also a botanist who sent plants back to his home in South Carolina where he had glasshouses.

In Mexico, poinsettias grow as tall garden plants and are called *La Flor de Nochebuena* – flower of the Holy Night – Christmas Eve, after a popular legend. A poor young girl had nothing to give the baby Jesus at the Christmas Eve church service. Her cousin told her that even the simplest gift from someone who loves Jesus would make him happy. She turned a handful of weeds picked from the roadside into a bouquet. As she placed this at the crib, the weeds burst into bright red flowers. All who witnessed this thought it was a miracle – hence their name.

DECK THE HALLS
Berry of Eternal Life

Holly growing as large shrubs in an American garden.

The tradition of decking the hall with boughs of holly can be traced back to ancient times. Holly symbolized fertility and eternal life for the druids, and cutting down a holly tree was thought to bring bad luck. But cutting holly branches and using them with other evergreens to decorate homes in winter was believed to bring good luck, and also signal that new life would follow in spring. To ancient Romans, holly was a symbol of Saturn, the god of agriculture, celebrated at the festival of Saturnalia lasting from 17th to 23rd December, when holly was hung above doorways to bring good fortune.

Lyrics of the popular carol 'Deck the Hall' were translated by Scottish musician Thomas Oliphant and first published in 1862. Its melody dates back to a 16-th century Welsh New Year's Eve carol 'Nos Galan'.

GARDENS' FESTIVE NIGHTS
Lit-Up Gardens

A Christmas spectacle at the Royal Botanic Gardens, Kew (see page 275).

Many large gardens install illuminations and light trails for the festive season that make evening visits a treat, even in the winter chill of the shortest days and longest nights – the winter solstice. Lights were an important part of both the Roman festival of Saturnalia and pagan celebrations at this time of year. This day marks the start of the New Year in the pagan calendar, where darkness turns to light as days begin to lengthen.

Night-time illumination gives a different perspective and a magical appearance to the well-known features and vistas of famous gardens. In domestic gardens, the simplest uplighting of a single tree can make any night of the year special.

CHRISTMAS TREE LIGHTS
A Decorating Tradition

A Christmas tree lit up outside the Manor at Bredon's Norton near Tewkesbury, UK.

American inventor Thomas Edison patented his incandescent light bulb in 1879. For Christmas 1880, he put together a string of lights and hung them across the entrance of his New Jersey laboratory to advertise his business. But it was Edison's friend and business partner Edward Johnson who hand-wired the first string of red, white and blue light bulbs and wound them around his Christmas tree at home in 1882 – the tree also rotated. They were expensive and several decades passed before more homes had electricity installed.

Also in the USA, the Sadacca family owned a novelty lighting company and in 1917, teenage son Albert suggested that their store should offer customers bright strings of Christmas tree lights, after a tragic fire caused by candles in New York City. True outdoor lights were a decade or so behind. Since 1998, Christmas tree lights are predominantly energy-efficient LEDs with longer lifetimes than their predecessors; they can also be recycled.

IT'S A WONDERFUL LIFE (1946)
A Wonderful Christmas Film

George Bailey speaks to his guardian angel, Clarence Odbody, on the steps of his home. We can see a Christmas wreath hanging on the inside of his front door.

Gardens are part of having a sense of home. Returning home for family celebrations is important to many people. When George Bailey is overwhelmed by his problems on Christmas Eve and wishes he had never been born, his guardian angel prevents his suicide and shows him what life would be like for his family, friends and hometown if he had never existed. The experience shows Bailey he has everything to live for, even if he loses material wealth, and begs his guardian angel to restore him to his real life. He is pleased to get back to his family and 'drafty' old home.

On its release in 1946, *It's a Wonderful Life* was not an immediate box-office success. Since its copyright lapsed, it has become one of the most popular Christmas films – one to rewatch every year.

CHRISTMAS WREATHS
Festive Front Doors

Two Christmas wreaths on a front door in Martha's Vineyard, Massachusetts, USA.

Wreaths originated in ancient Greek and Roman times and were used to denote competition winners, important statesmen and at entrances to important events. A circular shape with no beginning or end symbolizes eternal life in Christian traditions. In earlier times, taking greenery into homes and churches was a sign that spring – life in nature – would come again. Today, a front-door wreath is a way to extend inside decorations for the festive season to the outdoors, and to welcome people in for the celebrations.

SCHYNIGE PLATTE BOTANICAL ALPINE GARDEN, WILDERSWIL, SWITZERLAND
A Hibernating Garden

The garden in August, just a few months before it closes over winter. On this day, at the end of the year, the only visitors are hares and black grouse.

The only way to get to this garden is by the Schynige Platte Railway – a train ticket includes garden entry. Open from July to October, in winter it goes into hibernation under a blanket of snow, but alpine plants are adapted to these conditions and will return to their full glory the following year. It is a unique setting, at nearly 2,000m (6,500ft) above sea level, with over 750 plant species native to the Swiss Alps growing in natural communities against spectacular views of the Eiger, Mönch and Jungfrau. An alpine garden in a natural Alpine setting – the perfect combination, a thought to hold onto in the deep midwinter.

BLACK LAKE COTTAGE, SURREY, ENGLAND
Peter Pan's Garden

Three of the five Llewelyn-Davis boys acting for J.M.Barrie's *The Boy Castaways of Black Lake Island* in 1901.

Black Lake Cottage was the weekend home of author J. M. Barrie and his wife, Mary Ansell (see page 42). The Llewelyn-Davis family visited in the summer of 1901 and playing in the garden with their five sons prompted Barrie to create an imaginary world, full of adventure and drama. He captured some of their play in photographs and was inspired to write *Peter Pan*. The play was first performed on this day in 1904 at the Duke of York Theatre in London.

J. M. Barrie published two copies of a book *The Boy Castaways of Black Lake Island* about playing in the garden with the Llewelyn-Davis boys, with a preface by the middle son Peter, an inspiration for the character of Peter Pan. Only Barrie's copy remains in a private collection; Peter's parents, Sylvia and Arthur, mislaid theirs.

ROYAL BOTANIC GARDENS, SYDNEY, AUSTRALIA
The Calyx Installation

The interior of the Calyx glows against the end of a colourful Sydney sunset.

Located on the lands of the Cadigal peoples, this is Australia's oldest scientific institution and one of the oldest botanic gardens in the southern hemisphere. Cadi Jam Ora (First Encounters Garden) marks the site where newcomers from the First Fleet ships landed in 1788 and made their first attempts at farming introduced crops. While the garden's rich history began that year, its official foundation day was in 1816 when the Macquarie Road was completed.

To mark the bicentenary of the garden in 2016, commemorations included an installation by Aboriginal artist Jonathon Jones, *barrangal dyara (skin and bones)*, and the opening of the Calyx. This striking structure that represents the protective layer around a flower bud houses the garden's living collection and is a venue for education and special events. It is built on the site of a 1970s pyramid glasshouse. This historic yet forward-looking garden lies right in the heart of Sydney.

JOHN EVELYN IN HIS GARDEN (1937), GWEN RAVERAT
Holly Hedge Garden

English wood-engraver Gwen Raverat created this illustration for Geoffrey Keynes' study on John Evelyn, which was published in 1937. The original dimensions of the illustration were 15cm x 14.5cm.

John Evelyn was a writer, diarist and gardener. His travels after the English Civil War inspired his interest in European arts and sciences. On his return in 1653, he was appointed as one of the original council members of the Royal Society and created a renowned garden at his home, Sayes Court, close to the royal dockyard at Deptford.

Peter the Great stayed at the house while he studied shipbuilding at the dockyard in 1698. Considerable damage was inflicted during his stay. Evelyn's diary shows he was particularly upset by the destruction of his prized holly hedge, nurtured for around 20 years and supposedly 'impregnable' at 122m (400ft) long, 2.7m (9ft) high and 1.5m (5ft) deep. Peter and his entourage played a game that involved pushing people through the hedge in wheelbarrows. It must have been a very popular game – accounts say the hedge was flattened.

DESERT BOTANICAL GARDEN, PHOENIX, ARIZONA, USA
Las Noches de las Luminarias

Traditional *luminarias* add a special festive glow at Desert Botanical Garden.

Las Noches de las Luminarias at Desert Botanical Garden celebrates a Christmas tradition of lighting garden paths with *luminarias* during the nights just before and after Christmas. Strings of lights and musical performances add to the festive atmosphere on these evenings. *Luminarias* are traditional paper lantern bags weighted with sand and lit by votive lights, used for lighting pathways and delineating buildings. Their cultural origins stretch from Mexico to the Pueblos and Hispanos of New Mexico.

The Desert Botanical Garden also stays open into the night in warmer months for cooler garden visits when desert wildlife adds another dimension to its plants.

PRINCES STREET GARDENS, EDINBURGH, SCOTLAND
Gardens at Hogmanay

Fireworks illuminate the Princes Street Christmas Market on New Year's Eve. The gardens and streets surrounding are filled with musicians and other entertainers for the 100,000 revellers.

These gardens are an important urban park and tourists often name Princes Street as one of the most beautiful in the world. Princes Street Gardens separate the Old Town and the New Town and were created when one of Edinburgh's largest lochs, Loch Nor, was drained. From medieval times to the 19th century, the loch was said to be where 'witch ducking' took place.

In late November, the gardens are transformed into a lively winter wonderland with attractions including a Christmas Market, Christmas Wheel, Santa Land and all manner of seasonal treats. It is also the scene of the city's famous Hogmanay celebrations to bid farewell to the old year and welcome in the new.

INDEX

ACKNOWLEDGEMENTS

This book would not be possible without the skills and creativity of numerous people who have created, designed, built and planted extraordinary gardens around the world, and the teams that maintain gardens as they develop, age, or are restored. I am indebted to the many artists, photographers and writers whose work is inspired by gardens, and who, in turn, inspired me in the writing of this book. Many thanks to Tina Persaud for commissioning me to write this latest title in the '...A Day' series and a huge thank you to Kristy Richardson and Hattie Grylls for their editorial input. Finally, my love and thanks to my sister and brother-in-law, Judith and Kevin, for their support. A huge heartfelt thank you for listening to my ideas and discoveries throughout this project.

PICTURE CREDITS

Every effort has been made to contact the copyright holders. If you have any information about the images in this collection, please contact the publisher.

© The Estate of Evelyn Dunbar (Photograph Richard Valencia © Christopher Campbell-Howes) page 12 © Alamy Stock Photo / Carolyn Clarke pages 1, 170, 225; Joanna Kearney pages 4, 155; Philip Scalia pages 5, 109; Hemis pages 6, 88, 207, 347; Kevin Wheal pages 7, 270; Mark Mercer pages 8, 58; Lodge Photo pages 9, 38; Bailey-Cooper Photography pages 10, 202, 313, 321; John Bracegirdle pages 11, 35, 202, 218–9; Greg Balfour Evans page 13; PA Images pages 15, 115B, 153; gbimages page 16; SiliconValleyStock page 18; Matthew Taylor pages 19, 346B; Manfred Gottschalk page 21; robertharding pages 23, 62; World History Archive page 24; The Granger Collection page 25; Arctic Photo page 26T; Rolf_52 page 27; Pictorial Press Ltd pages 30, 247; Michael Wheatley page 32; DeGe Photo page 33; Fremantle page 34; Aracid Images page 36; mauritius images GmbH pages 37, 80, 114, 292; Peter Horree page 39; Michael Willis page 40; Tim Gainey page 41; gardenpics pages 44, 94, 231; Mikhail Slutsky pages 45; clu page 47; agefotostock pages 49, 226; Art Directors page 50; incamerastock page 51; View Stock page 52; Zuri Swimmer page 53; david pearson page 54; North Wind Picture Archives page 56; piemags/AAB page 60; David Stuckel page 61; paul prescott page 64; Scandphoto page 65; Michael Freeman page 66; jeremy sutton-hibbert page 67; TCD/Prod.DB pages 68, 235; H. Mark Weidman Photography page 70; Cavan Images page 72; Pocholo Calapre page 73; David Reed page 74; David H. Valle page 75; Carpe Diem UK page 76; Sen LI page 77; Stephen Dorey pages 78, 275; GL Archive page 79; James King-Holmes page 81; Danita Delimont pages 82, 239; Mark Bassett page 83B; The National Trust Photolibrary pages 85, 95, 284; SCFotos - Stuart Crump Photography 87; Richard Ellis page 89; The Print Collector page 91; Richard Barnes page 92; Herve Lenain page 93; Grant Heilman Photography page 96; PAINTING pages 97, 195; photo-fox page 99; Sandra Foyt page 102; Sebastian Wasek pages 104, 126 Tony Watson pages 105, 128; John Glover page 106; TOLBERT PHOTO page 107; Victor de Schwanberg page 111; Brian Lawrence page 112; Paul McErlane page 113; Flo Smith page 115T; earthjoy / Stockimo page 116; Classic Image page 118; DavidCC page 120; Rob Lavers Photography page 121; Steve Speller page 122; Helene ROCHE Photography page 125; Artepics pages 129, 255; Tim Cuff page 130;M Ramirez page 135; Linda Kennedy page 136; PRISMA ARCHIVO page 138; Richard Higgins page 139; Alex Ramsay pages 140, 223; Prisma by Dukas Presseagentur GmbH page 142B; ilpo musto page 143; Ian Dagnall pages 146, 163, 236, 244; Maximum Film page 147; Christian Evans page 149; Gordon Hulmes Travel page 150; aerial-photos.com page 151; Mike Booth page 154T; dave stamboulis page 154B; Anstock pages 156&7; Pat Tuson page 159T; Francois Roux page 160; Graham Prentice pages 161, 224; Chris Dorney page 168; Biblio Photography page 169; John Keates page 171; GAUTIER Stephane/SAGAPHOTO.COM page 173; Heritage Image Partnership Ltd pages

174, 303, 308, 311; Antiqua Print Gallery page 176; George Munday page 177; Raffaelo Cristofoli page 178; Allstar Picture Library Ltd page 179; Michael Hudson page 180; Aram Williams page 182; Kjersti Joergensen page 184; SilverScreen page 186; Zoonar GmbH page 188; John M. Chase page 190; Kristoffer Tripplaar page 191; D.G.Farquhar page 192; Jeremy Graham page 193; Laurence Jones/ljonesphotography.co.uk page 194; Ivan Vdovin page 196; flowerphotos page 197; Yagil Henkin page 200; Chris Lofty page 201B; The Artchives page 203; Andrew Lloyd page 204; IanDagnallComputing pages 208, 243B, 318; The Visual Pantry page 209; Ellen Rooney page 212; Bettina Strenske page 213; Josie Elias page 214; Universal Images Group North America LLC page 215; ian woolcock page 216; Chronicle page 220; Carol Barrington page 227; Christopher Nicholson pages 228, 317; Lebrecht Music & Art page 229T; Paul Quayle page 232; Nicholas Klein page 233; Andrey Khrobostov page 234; Eleni Mavrandoni page 241; Peter Barritt page 242; Peter Anderson page 245; Cannon Photography LLC page 248; Londonstills.com page 250; Alexandre ROSA page 251; Mirko Kuzmanovic page 252; M&N page 253; public domain sourced / access rights from Classic Graphics page 254; Stephen Bell page 256; Roy Johnson page 257; KGPA Ltd page 258; parkerphotography page 259; imageBROKER pages 261, 274, 304; Steven Sheppardson page 263; Peter Jordan_NE page 266; Martin Hughes-Jones page 268; Dellnesco page 269; David Humphreys page 271; INTERFOTO page 272; public domain sourced / access rights from The Picture Art Collection page 273B; Leonid Andronov page 276; Dariusz Gora page 277; John Smith page 278; Julian Krakowiac page 279; Rolf Richardson page 280; Bildarchiv Monheim GmbH page 281; Image Professionals GmbH page 282; Mark Ashbee page 288; Graeme Peacock page 289; Jerry Lai page 291T; Alexandre Rotenberg page 291B; Debussy page 294; Jeff Morgan 10 page 295; John Lander page 297; CBW page 298; Gordon Scammell page 299; V&A Images pages 300, 327; Neil McAllister page 301; David Crossland page 306; Sue Barr-VIEW page 307; public domain sourced / access rights from steeve-x-art page 310; Pat Canova page 315; Robert Hughes page 316; FORGET Patrick page 319; Image Professional GmbH page 322; Kenneth Taylor page 323; Air Video UK page 325; Hufton+Crow-VIEW page 326; funkyfood London – Paul Williams page 329; Thomas J Whitfield / Stockimo page 330; Steffen Hauser / botanikfoto page 331; Andrew Tryon page 334; John Carroll Photography page 336B; RM Floral page 337; Alexey Stiop page 341; steve blake page 343; Sid Frisby page 344; Ben Molyneux page 345; CuriousCatPhotos page 348; Sean Pavone page 350; William Perry 352; Rob Crandall page 353; Guy Corbishley page 354; naglestock.com page 355; Everett Collection Inc page 356; Mira page 357; Will Perrett page 358; Kenny McCartney page 363 © Estate of John Nash. All Rights Reserved 2020 / Bridgeman Images. Photo: Tate page 14

© Kenkoji Temple page 17 © Getty Images / Bettmann page 20; Dea, A. Dagli Orti page 29; clu page 47; Mirrorpix page 133; View Picture Limited page 134; Hulton Archive page 142T; Fine Art Images/Heritage Images page 240; page 312; Alessandro Rota page 332 © Bridgeman / The Estate of Ivon Hitchens. DACS 2023 page 22; Christie's Images page 31; CSG CIC Glasgow Museums Collection page 100; Michael Chase page 123; Christie's Images page 152; The Lucian Freud Archive page 165; British Library Board page 189; Collection Bourgeron page 309; Peter Graham page 314; Fry Art Gallery Society page 320, © Osborne & Little (www.osborneandlittle.com) page 26b; © Gap Photos / Richard Bloom pages 28, 249; John Glover page 148; Charles Hawes page 162; Marcus Harpur pages 201t, 205; Clive Nichols pages 287, 290; Abigail Rex page 296; © Timorous Beasties (www.timorousbeasties.com) page 42t © Flickr/ Picasa page 42b; Robert_Radlinski page 141 © Toowey's Antique & Fine Art Auctioneers & Valuers page 43 © Architectural Press Archive / RIBA Collections page 46 © Tom Stuart-Smith / Zoë Morris page 48; © Inge Morath / Magnum Photos 55t © Mary Evans Picture Library / Ashmolean Museum page 55b; pages 221, 232, 324; page 346; 351; © iStockPhoto / Brockswood page 57 © Maggie's Centres / Hufton+Crow page 59 © Richard Bloom page 69 © Dirk Heyman page 98 © Superstock/ Frank Lane Picture Agency page 101 © The Frick Collection, New York, 70th Street Garden / Michael Bodycomb page 103 © Shutterstock / G. J. Jurjens page 110; Mathilde Marest page 206 © Royal Collection Trust/His Majesty King Charles III page 117 © Clive Nichols page 127; page 132 © John Brookes-Denmans Foundation page 131 © Country Life Picture Library/ Time Inc (UK) Ltd page 13 © Rowley Hall Fine Art page 145 © National Trust Images/Andrew Butler pages 166–167; page 187; Simon Maycock page 293; Hufton+Crow page 335; Andrew Lawson pages 338–339 © Henry Ford Estate page 172b © Nigel Dunnett page 172t © Andrea Jones page 175 © Knepp Castle Estate page 181 © University of Oxford Botanic Garden and Arboretum page 210 © Colourised by Tom Marshall (PhotograFix) for the Little Museum of Dublin page 211 © Tate Images page 217; The Estate of Francis Bacon. DACS 2023. Page 285 © 2022 Heather Edwards page 222 © Andrew Lawson page 224 © Wiertn / Dreamstime.com page 229b © eyevine / Sophia Evans page 264 © Allan Pollok-Morris page 283 ©Esto /Peter Mauss page 320t ©Photography: Jason Busch/ Landscape architect: Vladimir Sitta page 328 © NASA page 333 © V&A Images page 336t © Betty Ford Alpine Gardens page 340t © The Dean and Chapter of Westminster page 340b © The Lamport Hall Preservation Trust / John Robertson Photos page 349 © Beinecke Rare Book and Manuscript Library page 359 © Botanic Gardens of Sydney page 360 © Estate of Gwen Raverat. All rights reserved, DACS 2023. Page 361